Positive English, Book 4

Positive English

Book 4

Albert Rowe

Macmillan Education

First published 1980

Published by
MACMILLAN EDUCATION LIMITED
Houndmills Basingstoke Hampshire RG21 2XS
and London
Associated companies in Delhi Dublin
Hong Kong Johannesburg Lagos Melbourne
New York Singapore and Tokyo

Filmset in Great Britain by
VANTAGE PHOTOSETTING CO. LTD
Southampton and London

Printed in Hong Kong

Contents

and cliches. Discussion. Written work. **Free verse: haiku and senrȳu.** Eight examples. **Writing and collecting haiku and senrȳu. Making sure: verse, rhyme, metre and rhythm.** 'Obituary', by Walt Mason. 'A Fact', by Bridget Muller. Written work. Essay topics.

(a) The semicolon. (b) The colon. (c) The single dash. (d) The hyphen.
Written work. Essay topics.

Unit 7   *98*

Prepositional usage. Language work. 'The Search', from *Citizen of the Galaxy*, by Robert A. Heinlein. Discussion. Written work. Answering comprehension questions on the extract. Punctuating a passage. Answering comprehension questions on the passage. Writing-up notes and making a précis. Spellings and vocabulary. Essay topics.

Unit 8   *110*

The language of business letters. Discussion on formal and informal language. **Hints on setting out and writing a business letter.** Discussion. Practice in writing business letters in appropriate language. Examples of unsatisfactory business letters. Discussion. Written work. **Making sure: using a pair of commas, dashes or brackets to enclose words in parenthesis.** (a) A pair of commas. (b) A pair of dashes. (c) A pair of brackets. Written work. Essay topics.

Unit 9   *125*

Describing and restricting adjective clauses. Discussion. Written work. **Personification.** Examples from Shakespeare, Shirley, Milton, Shelley, Browning, W. Hart-Smith. Discussion. Written work. **Onomatopoeia.** Discussion. Examples from Coleridge, Tennyson, William Morris, Stephen Spender. Written work. **Criticising a poem.** **Images and imagery.** Examples from Shakespeare, Donne, Keats, Byron, Browning, Swinburne, Alfred Noyes, Ted Hughes, Charles Causley. 'The River in March', by Ted Hughes. Discussion on imagery. Written work. 'My Mother Saw a Dancing Bear', by Charles Causley. Written work. **Making sure I: using the apostrophe.** **Making sure II: possessive pronouns.** Written work. Essay topics.

Unit 10   *142*

Common errors and confusions. Written work. **Test yourself.**

Unit 1

Inventing characters

Inventing characters, comic or serious, gives us the opportunity to
practise using language in a personal, lively, descriptive and
imaginative way.
  Here are three character studies in which language is used in this
subjective way.

'Thomas Gradgrind'

*The headmaster, Thomas Gradgrind, is explaining to Mr M'Choakumchild, the
new teacher, how he should teach.*

'Now, what I want is Facts. Teach these boys and girls nothing but
Facts. Facts alone are wanted in life. Plant nothing else, and root out
everything else. You can only form the minds of reasoning animals
upon Facts: nothing else will ever be of service to them. This is the
principle on which I bring up my own children, and this is the principle
on which I bring up these children. Stick to Facts, sir!'
  The scene was a plain, bare, monotonous vault of a schoolroom, and
the speaker's square forefinger emphasised his observations by
underscoring every sentence with a line on the schoolmaster's sleeve.
The emphasis was helped by the speaker's square wall of a forehead,
which had his eyebrows for its base, while his eyes found commodious
cellarage in two dark caves, overshadowed by the wall. The emphasis
was helped by the speaker's mouth, which was wide, thin, and hard set.
The emphasis was helped by the speaker's voice, which was inflexible,
dry, and dictatorial. The emphasis was helped by the speaker's hair,
which bristled on the skirts of his bald head, a plantation of firs to keep
the wind from its shining surface, all covered with knobs, like the crust

of a plum pie, as if the head had scarcely warehouse-room for the hard facts stored inside. The speaker's obstinate carriage, square coat, square legs, square shoulders—nay, his very neckcloth, trained to take him by the throat with an unaccommodating grasp, like a stubborn fact, as it was—all helped the emphasis.

'In this life, we want nothing but Facts, sir; nothing but Facts!'

The speaker, and the schoolmaster, and the third grown person present, all backed a little, and swept with their eyes the inclined plane of little vessels then and there arranged in order, ready to have imperial gallons of facts poured into them until they were full to the brim.

From Hard Times, by Charles Dickens

'My Uncle and His Wife'

I was staying at the time with my uncle and his wife. Although she was my aunt, I never thought of her as anything but the wife of my uncle, partly because he was so big and trumpeting and red-hairy and used to fill every inch of the hot little house like an old buffalo squeezed into an airing cupboard, and partly because she was so small and silk and quick and made no noise at all as she whisked about on padded paws, dusting the china dogs, feeding the buffalo, setting the mousetraps that never caught her; and once she sleaked out of the room, to squeak in a nook or nibble in the hayloft, you forgot she had ever been there.

But there he was, always, a steaming hulk of an uncle, his braces straining like hawsers, crammed behind the counter of the tiny shop at the front of the house, and breathing like a brass band; or guzzling and blustery in the kitchen over his gutsy supper, too big for everything except the great black boats of his boots. As he ate, the house grew smaller; he billowed out over the furniture, the loud check meadow of his waistcoat littered, as though after a picnic, with cigarette ends, peelings, cabbage stalks, birds' bones, gravy; and the forest fire of his hair crackled among the hooked hams from the ceiling. She was so small she could hit him only if she she stood on a chair, and every Saturday night at half past ten he would lift her up, under his arm, on to a chair in the kitchen so that she could hit him on the head with whatever was handy, which was always a china dog. On Sundays, and when pickled, he sang high tenor, and had won many cups.

From 'A Story', by Dylan Thomas

'Foggerty'

Foggerty wore a long, foul, ragged black overcoat, which seemed to have grown on him. It was secured round the middle with repeatedly-knotted string, from which hung various accoutrements, mug, hair-brush, spoon, fly-swat, tin-opener. An outsize greasy brown trilby, set low on his forehead, gave him the appearance of having no top to his head, which in fact he hadn't. Son of a long line of camp followers, he had been relieved of his post as lighthouse keeper at the Shale Rock when he drew the blinds, to 'stop the light shining down into the poor sailors' eyes'. The light was closed down, and these days ships have to find their own way on to the rocks. His father had been drowned after a brawl on the edge of a whisky vat, not that he couldn't swim; he tried to drink his way out. Alcoholic poisoning was the Coroner's verdict.

'I tell you, he was so beautifully preserved, it seemed a shame ter bury him,' said the amazed mortician.

From *Puckoon*, by Spike Milligan

Discussion

The painter Vincent Van Gogh once said that the art of painting a portrait was to exaggerate the essential. How does this statement apply to the portraits in words created by Dylan Thomas, Charles Dickens and Spike Milligan?

Compare the methods the three writers use to achieve their effects. For instance, what physical details of the characters' faces, bodies and clothing are we given, and what details are left to our imagination? In what ways do the physical details that we are given reveal the character of the person concerned?

What actions are mentioned? What is revealed to us through the writer's choice of which actions to mention, and the way he describes them?

Study the pattern of the sentences—their length, punctuation, and the way the words are arranged in them. Discuss how the patterns reinforce the effect the words have on us, e.g. Dickens's reiteration of the phrase, 'the emphasis was helped', and the poet Dylan Thomas's use of alliteration.

Compare these techniques with those used in ballads, old and new.

Discuss also Dylan Thomas's use of similes and metaphors, and in particular how he rapidly switches from one metaphor to another for comic effect.

Which passage did you enjoy most, and why?

Written work

1 Taking hints from the Dylan Thomas passage, write comic but affectionate character studies of these fictitious persons:
(a) a grandfather or grandmother who was the funniest person you have ever known;
(b) a zany pupil who is constantly in trouble at school;
(c) the thinnest or fattest person you knew when you were a child.

2 Taking hints from the Dickens passage, write imaginative character studies of these fictitious persons, which will clearly convey through the language you use your feelings about them:

(a) a teacher you once hated;

(b) a cruel relative;

(c) the person of your own age you dislike the most.

3 Use the Spike Milligan passage as your inspiration and write comic character sketches of:

(a) a tramp;

(b) a student dropout;

(c) a busker;

(d) a very eccentric old woman who lives with a houseful of cats.

Writing accurate descriptions of people

To write an *accurate* description of someone, we must have keen powers of observation, a good memory, and be able to convey what we have seen and remembered in clear, impersonal factual prose. Such a description is objective, not subjective.

On the following page is part of a form the police use to help them make an accurate physical description of a wanted person.

Discussion

Go through the part of the form reproduced on the following page, choose one adjective from each group that applies to yourself and jot it down.

In your own opinion and that of others, do the adjectives in your list give a brief but complete picture of you? If not, what other headings and adjectives would you like to add to those in the form to make the picture complete, and why?

The adjectives on the form are used in this way: a policeman can choose any he wishes, or substitute or add adjectives of his own. There is also a space on the complete form for extra information, though there are no more headings.

Amuse yourselves by using the form to build up oral descriptions of the people in the photographs on page 15. Do you always agree on which adjective to use to describe a particular feature? Why?

HEIGHT.....................................
LOOKS TALLER OR SHORTER

BUILD...
PROPORTIONATE: STOUT: CORPULENT: HEAVY: THICK-
SET: THIN: SLIM: WELL-BUILT: MILITARY BEARING:
SLOUCHES: ERECT: STOOPS: ROUND-SHOULDERED.

COMPLEXION.............................
FRESH: RUDDY: FLORID: PALE: SALLOW: BLOTCHY:
PIMPLY: USES COSMETICS.

FACE...
ROUND: OVAL: LONG: WRINKLED: FLABBY: FAT: THIN:
HIGH CHEEK-BONES: EXPRESSION – VACANT:
SCOWLING: PLEASANT.

HAIR.......................................
TURNING GREY: GOING BALD: WAVY: PERMANENTLY
WAVED: STRAIGHT: CURLY: FRIZZY: PARTED:
UNPARTED: BRUSHED BACK: LONG: SHORT: HOW CUT:
GREASED: UNKEMPT: WEARS WIG: BLEACHED: DYED.

HAIR ON FACE.............................
BEARD (SHAPE AND COLOUR): MOUSTACHE (SIZE,
SHAPE, COLOUR, WAXED): DARK CHIN: SIDEBOARDS.

HEAD..
LARGE: SMALL: NARROW: SQUARE.

FOREHEAD....................................
HIGH: LOW: BROAD: NARROW: WRINKLED: BULGING:
RECEDING.

EYEBROWS.................................
THICK: THIN: BUSHY: PLUCKED: PENCILLED: ARCHED:
SPARSE: MEET IN CENTRE.

EYES...
CAST: BLIND: MISSING: GLASS: RED RIMMED: LONG
LASHES: EYELASHES DROOP: SPECTACLES (FOR
READING OR HABITUALLY – HORN-RIMMED): PINCE-
NEZ: BI-FOCAL: SHAPE OF LENS/FRAME.

NOSE.......................................
LARGE: SMALL: LONG: SHORT: HOOKED: IRREGULAR:
TURNED UP: ROMAN: BROKEN: BULBOUS: BROAD BASE:
WIDE OR NARROW NOSTRILS.

MOUTH.....................................
LARGE: SMALL: HABITUALLY OPEN: CLOSE SHUT.

LIPS..
THICK: THIN: LOOSE: HARE-LIP: WELL-SHAPED: UPPER
OR LOWER PROTRUDES. *Medium*

TEETH......................................
CLEAN: DISCOLOURED: DECAYED: WIDELY SPACED:
IRREGULAR: DENTURES: FILLINGS: GAPS: GOLD:
CROWNED: TOOTHLESS: OVERLAP.

CHIN.......................................
DIMPLED: CLEFT: DOUBLE: POINTED: ROUND:
PROTRUDES: RECEDES: SQUARE JAW.

EARS.......................................
LARGE: SMALL: PROTRUDE: CAULIFLOWER: LOBELESS:
LARGE LOBES: PIERCED.

HANDS......................................
LONG: SHORT: BROAD: LONG FINGERS: SHORT
FINGERS: ROUGH: NAILS – LONG: SHORT: BITTEN:
DIRTY: MANICURED: VARNISHED.

VOICE.......................................
ACCENT: GRUFF: MELODIOUS: HIGH-PITCHED: DEEP:
LOUD: SOFT: EFFEMINATE: AFFECTED: LISP: STAMMER
OR OTHER IMPEDIMENT: DIFFICULTY WITH CERTAIN
WORDS.

14

a) b)

c) d)

e) f)

g) h)

Written work

1   Choose any five people from the photographs. Copy the headings
    from the police form, and opposite each put the appropriate
    adjective.
2   Use this information to write an accurate, impersonal, factual
    description of each person.

Blue

3   Write complete and objective physical descriptions of:
     (a) yourself (use a mirror if you wish);
     (b) three members of your family;
     (c) two of your best friends.
4   Write similarly objective, but unnamed, descriptions of:
     (a) a pupil in your form;
     (b) a pupil in any other form;
     (c) two members of staff.
5   Test the objectivity and factual accuracy of your descriptions by
     asking other members of your form to name the persons you have
     described in No. 4. Write up the results of the test, giving reasons
     for your successes and failures.

Discussion: comparing the language used in inventing characters with that used to write factual descriptions of actual people

Compare the subjective language Dylan Thomas, Charles Dickens and
Spike Milligan use to create their fictitious characters with the
objective language you yourselves have used to write your factual
physical descriptions of people. Suppose, for example, you had to fill in
the police form from the Thomas, Dickens and Milligan passages. How
many actual facts do the writers provide about the characters they have
created? Despite this, would you feel reasonably sure of recognising
Uncle, Gradgrind and Foggerty if you saw them? Why?

What evidence could be put forward for the statement that all three
writers based their fictitious characters on real people, then
'exaggerated the essential', then added details from other real-life
characters?

Written work

1   Imagine that you knew Uncle, Aunt, Gradgrind and Foggerty.
     Make brief notes of what they actually looked like, using all the
     form headings, and the appropriate adjectives from the lists.
2   Write in plain, factual prose accurate and complete physical
     descriptions of all four characters.

16

3   Carefully explain what a reader would miss by reading your objective descriptions rather than the subjective originals.
4   Suppose that someone was asked to identify all four of them. Would your descriptions or the original passages provide the better guide, and why?
5   Two people are coming to stay with you. You ask a friend to meet these persons for you at a busy railway station. Write, in clear, accurately punctuated prose, descriptions which will enable the persons to be easily recognised.
6   Write a letter to a friend inviting her/him to stay with you for a week and outlining how you will spend your time. Include the usual greetings to her/his family and news of yourself and your family.
7   Draw an envelope 15 cm by 11 cm and address it to your friend as the Post Office recommends.

Writing reviews and forming a reviewers circle

Books of all kinds are regularly reviewed in many newspapers and magazines. A satisfactory review fulfils two purposes:
    i. it gives readers an adequate idea of what the book being reviewed is about;
    ii. it offers a reasoned opinion of the strengths and weaknesses of the book—of how good it is of its kind.
    Writing reviews gives us excellent practice in using language correctly, appropriately and fluently. To fulfil the first purpose of the review, we must give a clear and factually accurate account of the book. To fulfil the second, we must state with our reasons our personal opinion of it, supported where necessary by suitable quotations.
    Language practice is much more valuable if it is regular and sustained, as is practice in any skill. One way to ensure this is to form a *Reviewers Circle*. Members could review, say, one work of fiction a month, as well as some works of non-fiction if they wish. They could choose books from school or public library, or from among those they own. The reviews could be published (displayed or made available in some other way) to help others decide what book to read next.

Two or more members of the circle could sometimes read and review the same book, and compare their reviews. Other members who have read a book reviewed could also from time to time meet and compare their own opinion of the book with that of the reviewer.

The best way of increasing our ability to speak and write English correctly, appropriately and fluently is to read good books. This is true, however much we are taught about the English language, and however many written exercises we do.

When we read a book for our own pleasure, we certainly absorb some of the language without being conscious of it, and this helps us to increase our own command of spoken and written language. When, however, we read a book as critically and attentively as a reviewer does, we absorb some of the language consciously as well as unconsciously, and this helps us even more to increase our command of language, especially of written language.

Discussion

Why do publishers send new books to newspapers and magazines in the hope that they will be reviewed?

Only a tiny percentage of the books sent for review are ever reviewed. How, then, do publishers bring all the books they publish to the attention of possible readers?

Talk about the various ways in which we get to know about what programmes, films and exhibitions are being put on, and what new records are being produced.

Discuss in detail how you decide what book to read next, what kinds of books you like and who your favourite authors are.

A good way of preparing to write a review of a work of fiction is to begin by jotting down the questions you yourself would want to have answered. Here are some to consider; no doubt you can add others of your own. What kind of story is it? Is the setting rural, urban, familiar, modern, historical, unusual, strange? Is the story well plotted and easy to follow? What kind of beginning and ending has it? Is it fast-moving—interesting, exciting, very exciting? Is the language easy or difficult to understand? Who are the chief characters? Are they convincing and true to life? Is the dialogue natural and interesting? How does the story compare with others of its kind?

Now criticise this review written by a pupil of your own age. Remember that when the word 'criticise' is applied to a written work, it means discussing the good points as well as the bad.

A review of 'Mike and Me', by David Line, Puffin, 139 pages

If you read and enjoyed *Run for Your Life*, as I did, then you will probably enjoy David Line's new book, especially if you are a boy.

The teller of the story is Jim Woolcott, the boy who told the story in *Run for Your Life*. This time the pal who shares his adventures is not Soldier, but his cousin, Mike Mitchell. Soldier is in the story as well, but he only has a small part in it.

Mike is fifteen, one year older than Jim, but in the same class. He is over six feet tall, will do anything rather than get in a fight, but if he did get into a fight he is so strong he could flatten anybody. Though he is not very quick in thinking things out, he often guesses what is going to happen before Jim, who is much cleverer, can work it out. This is a good job for both of them, because his instinct and not Jim's reasoning saves them both more than once. Mike, not Jim, is the real hero of the story, and I liked him very much.

The first part of the story takes place in their school, where there is a 'nutty' art master, a 'swine' of a headmaster, and a 'twit' of a woodwork master, who is always picking on Jim. Despite one master's plot to try to get Mike expelled, this part of the story did not interest me very much.

The main part of the story is about a bunch of speculators who want to pull down the old part of the town, and put up skyscrapers to make a huge profit. Moggy, the 'nutty' art master, finds an old document which will prevent the town council from selling this old part of the town. The speculators get to know about the document, and make up their minds to do something about it. David Line takes up quite a number of pages explaining the importance of the document, and this I also found a bit boring.

The rest of the story I found as exciting as anything I have read for quite a while. The document disappears, the art master is nearly killed, and Mike and Jim have to run for their lives. How and why all this happens I will leave you to find out for yourself.

One thing I was impressed by was the way David Line tells the story in the sort of words and slang a boy of fourteen would use. Except in the first part of the story, as I have said, he does not stop to describe or explain anything, but gets on with the action. Everything happens at a great speed, and this is what I like.

There are no pictures in this book. I am glad, as I prefer to imagine what the characters look like.

Robert

Written work

1 Write a personal criticism of Robert's review, putting forward what you consider its good points as well as its bad, and adding what else you would have liked to be included.
2 Write a review between two and three pages long of a work of fiction you have read recently. If necessary, first reread the work

and take brief notes. Include in your title the same details as Robert included in his.

3 Write a similar review of the work of fiction you are currently reading.

4 Put forward your own views on fiction written chiefly for girls or for boys. In your own experience, is there a reasonable balance between the two? If not, why not? Is the book you reviewed in No. 3 more likely to be reviewed by girls or by boys, and why? Point out the features in other stories you have read recently which make them more suitable for girls or for boys.

5 Choose a non-fiction book from the library on a subject in which you are interested, and write a review of it. Be sure to include some assessment of these points:
(a) how up-to-date and accurate the text is;
(b) the type and difficulty of language used;
(c) the kind, quality and relevance of the illustrations and diagrams;
(d) the kind of cover and its appearance, and how well the book is bound;
(e) the quality of the paper and of the typefaces used.

6 Write a similar review of a one-volume encyclopedia with which you are familiar.

7 Write reviews of:
(a) a TV play you have watched recently;
(b) a TV series you have watched recently;
(c) a film.

8 Write a review of an exhibition, in school or out, that you have visited. The first part of the review should consist of a detailed and factual report on the exhibition (the objective part), and the second of your personal opinion of it and feelings about it (the subjective part).

Writing an essay

In this book, we shall use the word 'essay' rather than the word 'composition' to refer to a piece of writing in prose of approximately three to six pages in length.

In many essays we do not use the pronoun 'I', nor directly express any personal views. To be successful, however, even such essays will convey something of our own personality to the reader. Whatever the subject, an essay is a subjective piece of writing: in it we can be ourselves.

An essay question forms an important part of the English Language paper, because it gives candidates an excellent opportunity to demonstrate their command of language. Even if we do not intend to sit that examination, practising writing essays will help us:

i. to improve our ability to use language to tell a story, write a description, conduct a discussion or an argument, and to write easily and entertainingly on a wide variety of topics;

ii. to plan and organise our ideas before we begin to write so that we can express them appropriately and effectively, for planning is one of the keys to successful essay-writing.

Make a habit for a time of discussing and planning the essay topics together before you choose one. This will be an important step in enabling you later to write a good essay entirely on your own.

For those of you who will be taking an examination in English language in the future, each list of topics contains various types of essays—narrative, descriptive, argumentative, discursive. By deliberately choosing some from each type, you will, with your teacher's help, gradually discover which you do best. These will probably be the ones you most enjoy doing.

Essay topics

1 'A good education is more important for a boy than a girl.' Discuss.
2 Relate and comment on the recent newspaper story that interested you most.
3 Photography.
4 Dreams and daydreams.
5 Interesting People I Have Known.
6 Describe a great occasion in sport.

Unit 2

The value of comprehension questions and detailed hints on how to answer them

Comprehension questions test our understanding of a passage, and our ability to show that we understand it by writing correct answers to the questions set on it.

Practice in answering comprehension questions:

i. improves our general command of language;

ii. gives us training in the best techniques to use in answering such questions;

iii. accustoms us to the close and careful study of a written passage, something we often have to do in our everyday lives.

Study and discuss these hints on how to tackle comprehension questions. Some of the hints will be familiar, others will be new.

1   Read the passage through quickly to get the general sense. Do not linger over, or be dismayed by, unfamiliar words (see No. 8).

2   Read the passage again, this time very carefully. This will enable you to grasp the general sense of the passage, and to ascertain what the main topic or topics are.

3   Read equally carefully the questions and the instructions on answering them, so that you thoroughly understand both.

4   Write your answers in your own words in complete, correctly punctuated sentences. The wording of the question will often guide you on how to begin your answer.

5   While writing an answer, keep referring as often as is necessary to the part of the passage on which the answer is based to check that you are getting your facts right. (This includes the spelling of unfamiliar words!)

6   Make the content of your answer as complete as possible. Include everything the question asks for, even though you may feel that some of it is too obvious to be worth mentioning.

7   Remember that you may need to search the whole passage to find all the facts needed for your answer. Do not, however, include facts not mentioned in the passage, unless the question specifically asks for them.
8   Use the context to help you to deduce the meaning of unfamiliar words. It is better to write down your deduction than to leave the question unanswered—you may well be right!
9   When asked to reason out something from the facts, a careful study of the whole context may help you to reason correctly.

'Paella'

More and more Europeans, young and old, as well as entire families, are now spending their holidays in Spain, mostly on the Costa Brava, the Costa Blanca and the Costa del Sol. The chief attractions, needless to say, are the abundant sunshine, the warm sea of the Mediterranean, and the cheap booze and cigarettes.

When we come to food, it is another matter. The popular myth is that if you eat Spanish food you get Spanish tummy. The reason, so the myth has it, is that Spanish food is very greasy and reeks of garlic. This is a total misconception: nothing could be further from the truth. Spanish food is invariably cooked in olive oil—yes, that is a fact. But olive oil is a very pure vegetable oil. It is far less greasy than lard or butter or any combination of animal and vegetable oil, and is far more easily digestible.

Spanish hotel proprietors soon realised that foreigners were prejudiced against their national food, so they evolved a menu which could offend no one, adjusted according to the nationality of their guests. If you want to eat real Spanish food, you must go to restaurants where the Spaniards themselves eat. The best of these are often situated in narrow back streets, have somewhat unprepossessing exteriors, but inside is another matter! I have often asked myself why so many of the most desirable restaurants are situated in such streets, and look so shabby outside. Perhaps it is simply that the proprietor does not want to attract tourists, beacause he has enough regular Spanish customers already, and neither would his regulars want to be crowded out by foreigners.

The most famous of all Spanish dishes is 'paella', pronounced *pah-eh-ya*, with the stress on the *eh*. At its best, this is a dish that once eaten, is never forgotten. It is brought to the table in a splendid, black, iron frying-pan full of hot, yellow savoury rice, liberally sprinkled with crayfish, prawns, squid, mussels, octopus, chicken and pork, topped up with sliced tomato, egg, and green peppers.

Such a paella is a meal in itself—and more than a meal for most of us! To the Spaniard, however, it is only one dish in the usual three-course meal: soup, mixed salad or hors d'oeuvre; paella, fish, chicken, pork, or steak, the latter four served with abundant vegetables; dessert and coffee. But the Spaniards take their food seriously, and a meal like this commonly lasts three or four hours. Where better to spend the hottest part of the day than in a cool restaurant, lingering over carefully-prepared, delicious food, in the company of one's family and friends? After all, the next meal is not due until after 10 p.m.!

Anthony Everton

Discussion on paragraphs, punctuation and parts of speech

Remind yourselves of the reasons for dividing prose into paragraphs.
What main topic does each of Anthony Everton's paragraphs deal with? Sum up each topic in a few words.

Identify the sentences in which there are words in parenthesis. How are they separated from the main sentence?

Look at the sentences beginning with 'When' and 'If' (paras 2 and 3). How are the words which follow them separated from the main sentence? When we begin sentences with such words, what are they a reminder to us to do?

Pick out the conjunctions which link one clause to another. How are the clauses separated from each other?

Study the use of commas in the sentence beginning 'It is brought to the table . . .'. What units of meaning are the commas used to separate?

What effects do the single dashes and the exclamation marks achieve (paras 2 and 5)?

Explain the use of the colon in the fourth sentence in paragraph 2, and the colon and semicolons in the second sentence of the last paragraph.

What part of speech is each of the two compound words, and what is used to link them?

Check that you can identify examples of the various parts of speech, and explain the work they do in their sentences.

Imitating model sentences and answering comprehension questions

1   Copy three of the sentences containing words in parenthesis, but substitute words in parenthesis of your own.
2   Copy two of the same sentences. This time, use two other forms of punctuation marks to separate the words in parenthesis from the main sentence. What effect have your alterations achieved?
3   Write a sentence about an English dish, in which you use commas for the same purpose as in the sentence describing *paella*.
4   Write sentences of your own modelled on those in which a single dash is used.

5   Write a sentence modelled on the second sentence in the last paragraph, in which you use a colon and semicolons for the same purpose.

6   What synonyms could be substituted for these in the first paragraph? Europeans, entire, needless to say, booze.

7   What are the chief attractions of Spain for European holiday-makers?

8   What is a myth?

9   What myth is referred to in the second paragraph? Why is it believed by so many people?

10 Explain the meaning of 'total misconception' and 'invariably' (para. 2).

11 What advantages has olive oil over other kinds of cooking oils?

12 Use 'prejudiced against' in a sentence which will show its meaning.

13 What is a 'desirable' restaurant?

14 Mention the points that would make a restaurant a desirable one to you.

15 Explain in your own words the reasons Anthony Everton put forward for some desirable restaurants being situated in back streets, and looking so shabby outside.

16 What synonyms could be substituted for these (para. 3)? proprietors, evolved, adjusted, unprepossessing, exteriors, situated, shabby, regulars.

17 Use the words themselves in sentences which will make clear their meaning.

18 Explain fully what the phrase 'inside is another matter' (para. 3) conveys to you.

19 What are the antonyms of: myth, misconception, invariably, vegetable, digestible, foreigners, prejudiced, savoury, latter?

20 Use the antonyms in sentences that will clearly illustrate their meaning.

21 How would you *liberally* sprinkle something (para. 4)?

22 Use 'liberally' in a sentence which will demonstrate the meaning it has in its context.

23 Explain, with examples: (a) hors d'oeuvre; (b) dessert.

24 Use both words in sentences to show their meaning.

25 Give the passage a suitable alternative title.

Spelling and spelling rules

Being able to spell words correctly is not a matter of life or death: it is, however, of some importance. Remind yourselves of the reasons for making the greatest possible effort to spell correctly the words you use.

In the section *Spellings and vocabulary* we will concentrate on words which, for one reason or another, are often misspelled, as well as on difficult words used in previous units.

Where a spelling rule may help you to avoid future mistakes, we will deal with it. Some of the rules will be new, some you will have met before.

There are four other measures you can take to improve your spelling.

1   Your chief spelling aid is the dictionary. Remember always to check the spelling of any word you are unsure of before you write it. It is much easier to go on spelling a word correctly if you spell it correctly the first time you use it.

2   Check your spelling before you hand in your written work, and correct any misspellings.

3   Keep a notebook. Enter the correct spelling of words you have misspelled. Draw your own attention to the troublesome letters by writing them in capitals or in colour. When revising the words, put the emphasis on the troublesome letters. Take special care when writing these words until you are sure you can spell them correctly.

4   Always correct spelling mistakes marked by your teacher. The ones you commonly make should be entered in your notebook and learned.

The spelling rules for using ful *as a suffix or prefix*

i.   When *full* is used as a suffix to make another word, it is spelled *-ful*: hopeful, thoughtful, spoonful, careful, pocketful, wonderful, watchful, bashful, wakeful, tactful, cupful, joyful, awful.

ii.   When *-ful* is added to a word ending in *y*, the *y* is changed to *i*: beautiful, pitiful, bountiful, dutiful.

iii.   When *-ful* is added to a word ending in *ll*, one *l* is dropped: skilful, wilful.

iv. When *full* is used as a prefix, it is spelled *ful-*: fulfil, fulsome.

v. Note the spelling of adverbs like these, formed by adding the suffix *-ly* to the suffix *-ful*: beautifully, tactfully, skilfully, thoughtfully.

Spellings and vocabulary

1 Test with your neighbour that you can spell all the above words. Learn those you misspelled, then test yourselves again.

2 Use the words you misspelled in interesting sentences. (Check that you have spelled the words correctly.)

3 Use these adjectives correctly spelled, in sentences that will clearly demonstrate their meaning: bashful, tactful, pitiful, bountiful, dutiful, skilful, wilful, careful, hopeful, wonderful.

4 Write the adverbial form of those adjectives.

5 Use the adverbs, correctly spelled, in interesting sentences.

6 These words have been used in Units 1 and 2.

I	II	III	IV
criticise	buffalo	hawsers	guzzling
blustery	ate	Saturday	tenor
monotonous	vault	emphasised	observations
sentence	emphasis	commodious	inflexible
dictatorial	obstinate	unaccommodating	accoutrements
relieved	beautifully	mortician	exaggerate
affectionate	fictitious	pencilled	corpulent
flabby	receding	habitually	cauliflower
straightforward	Europeans	Mediterranean	misconception
invariably	digestible	unprepossessing	savoury
liberally	hors d'oeuvre	dessert	bachelor

(a) Take the words one column at a time and test with your neighbour that you can spell them correctly.

(b) Learn those you misspelled, test yourselves again, and enter in your notebook those you think may give you future trouble, revising them regularly.

7 Use these words in sentences which will clearly demonstrate their meaning: hawser, vault, emphasis, commodious, dictatorial,

mortician, accoutrements, corpulent, habitually, liberally, hors
d'oeuvre.
8   Write these words and their antonyms: blustery, monotonous,
inflexible, unaccommodating, fictitious, receding, digestible,
unprepossessing, savoury, bachelor.
9   Use these words themselves in sentences that will clearly illustrate
their meaning.

Most of the following sections cover in a different way the uses of all the
punctuation marks we have dealt with in the course, as well as some
uses that will be new to you.
    Thoroughly discuss the sections, then work through them carefully
and conscientiously.

Making sure I: the essential parts of a sentence

1   Define a sentence.
2   Of what two parts must a complete sentence consist?
3   By adding as little as you can, turn each of these into the shortest
possible sentence: (a) They; (b) Molly and Jill; (c) We; (d) slept;
(e) shouted; (f) is digging; (g) will have been here.
4   What part did you add to make each of the above into a sentence?
5   Distinguish between a sentence and a phrase.
6   Pick out and write down five phrases from Anthony Everton's
piece (pp. 24−6).
7   Make each phrase into a complete sentence of your own.

Making sure II: the use of capital letters

Capital letters are used:
  i. To begin the first word of a sentence.
 ii. To begin the first word in direct speech.
iii. To begin a proper noun naming a particular person or thing, and
an initial when it stands for a proper noun.
 iv. To begin the important words of titles of particular persons,
buildings, films, books, magazines, songs, poems and paintings.

v. For the pronoun *I*, and for pronouns referring to God, Jesus, Buddha and Mohammed.

1 Copy these sentences, correcting the misuse of capital letters.

   (a) He said, 'we believe in god the father, and that he is all-powerful.'

   (b) The greeks and Romans had many gods, each with His or Her own temple and cult.

   (c) 'in my opinion,' she said solemnly, 'all titles of persons such as Dukes, Duchesses, Lords and Ladies, add a little welcome colour to our drab lives.'

   (d) She could see that father was very cross when he entered the room, but mother took not the slightest notice.

2 Write the proper nouns used in paragraph 1 of Anthony Everton's piece (p. 24).

3 Use three of the nouns in interesting sentences of your own.

4 Write the correct version of this sentence: the mediterranean sea is an inland, tideless sea.

5 What adjective is written with a capital letter in paragraph 2 of Anthony Everton's piece on page 24, and why?

6 Write three other adjectives formed from the name of people who live in a particular country.

7 Use those adjectives in interesting sentences.

8 Reread paragraph 1 of the Dylan Thomas extract (p. 9), then write sentences in which you use these phrases: (a) his father and mother; (b) our uncle and aunt; (c) my grandparents.

9 Copy these sentences, correcting the use of capital letters:

   (a) we asked uncle where he was going.

   (b) 'where are you going, uncle?' we asked.

   (c) Both his Father and Mother are here.

   (d) neither grandma nor grandpa can come.

10 Use capital letters to write correctly the name of: (a) a saint; (b) one of God's prophets; (c) three persons you know; (d) two persons and their titles; (e) a building; (f) an ocean; (g) a popular song; (h) a book; (i) a car; (j) a soft drink.

11 Use any four of the names in interesting sentences.

12 Use the name of the author of *Hard Times*, and of the two schoolmasters involved in the extract from it (pp. 9 and 10), in an interesting paragraph, taking care to spell all three names correctly.

Making sure III: the contractions used in informal writing and in writing conversations

These are the commonest contractions. Discuss with your teacher in what kinds of informal writing it is appropriate to use them.

I'm — I am
you're — you are
she's — she is
he's — he is
we're — we are
they're — they are
I've — I have
can't — cannot
wasn't — was not
doesn't — does not
you've — you have

I'll — I will
you'll — you will
she'll — she will
it'll — it will
he'll — he will
we'll — we will
they'll — they will
won't — will not
weren't — were not
don't — do not
we've — we have

I'd — I would
you'd — you would
she'd — she would
it'd — it would
he'd — he would
we'd — we would
they'd — they would
wouldn't — would not
let's — let us
shan't — shall not
there'll — there will

1   Test with your neighbour that you can write the contraction when the two words themselves are said to you.
2   Learn those you got wrong, and retest yourselves.
3   Use the correct form of the contractions you got wrong in sentences containing conversation.
4   Write the conversation the people are having in the photograph on page 33. Include yourself in the group if you wish, and use as many contractions as possible.

Essay topics

1   Road Safety.
2   Pets.
3   Give an account of your favourite entertainment, It may be a sport, the cinema, television, music, reading, dancing—or something else. State why it appeals to you more than other forms of entertainment.
4   Describe a holiday you enjoyed.
5   My Earliest Childhood Memories.
6   'Monarchy is an anachronism.' Discuss.

Unit 3

Changing direct into reported (indirect) speech

Questions on changing direct into reported speech are often set in
examinations, because they are a useful way of testing how accurately
and efficiently we can use language.

Though we use the reported speech form easily and correctly in our
everyday conversations, we sometimes find difficulty in changing a
written passage from direct to reported speech. This is because it is an
artificial exercise—we are substituting a conscious for an unconscious
process.

Discussion

Listen carefully while this little story is read to you. Retell it to your
neighbour, as you naturally would if you were repeating it to someone
who had not heard it before, then work out in detail the changes you
unconsciously made in putting the direct into reported speech. This is
the key to changing direct into reported speech.

People on market day used to offer Charlie, the local beggar, two coins,
one of lesser and one of greater value. Charlie always took the one of
lesser value.

'Why, Charlie, why on earth do you always take the coin that isn't
worth as much as the other?' his friend once asked him in bewilderment.

'Ah, Tom,' Charlie said, 'if I took the one you think I should, people
would stop giving me anything.'

'But why? I just don't see it!'

'Because,' replied Charlie, grinning broadly at his friend's
astonishment, 'they only offer me two coins to see me take the one not
worth as much as the other. Do you get it now?'

'No, I don't.'

'Well, when they see me take the one I always do, they know I'm a bigger fool than they are, and they go away happy.'

Detailed hints on changing direct to reported speech

1   Do not use quotation marks—you are not quoting the actual words, but only their general sense.

2   Change direct to indirect questions. This means that any question marks disappear.

3   Introduce the general sense of each remark by a phrase containing 'that' or 'which', e.g. Martin said that . . .

4   Change the tense of the verbs, e.g. from present to past.

5   Change 1st and 2nd person pronouns to 3rd person, e.g. *I* to *he/she*; *we* to *they*; *us* to *them*. (Also *you/me* to *I* when the context demands it.)

6   Change possessive adjectives and pronouns in the same way, e.g. *my* to *his/her*; *mine* to *his/hers*; *our* to *their*; *ours* to *theirs*; *your* to *their*; *yours* to *theirs*.

7   Change conversational contractions to their full form, e.g. *can't* to *cannot*.

8   Substitute acceptable written forms for conversational slang, and for interjections, e.g. *'Ouch!' he said, 'that hurt'* could become *He cried out sharply that it had hurt him*.

9   Words such as *here, now, this, today, yesterday* become *there, then, the day before*.

10   To avoid the monotony of repeating 'said that' too many times, vary it according to the sense, e.g. *told, reminded*.

Written work

1   Rewrite these sentences, changing the direct to reported speech.

(a) 'The concert starts promptly at seven,' Mohammed said.
(b) 'Are you going to the concert, Paul?' said Tony.
(c) 'Where have I left my bag, Mother?' said Tina.
(d) Gita said, 'We will stay here, but they can go if they wish.'
(e) 'My ball has been lost,' Bob said. 'Shall we play with yours?'
(f) 'It isn't here now,' said Carole. 'I wonder if they took it yesterday?'
(g) 'This is ours. We bought it this morning. Yours was here yesterday, but it seems to have disappeared,' Gary said.
(h) 'She's fed up to the teeth with her job, and has made up her mind to chuck it in,' Heather said.
(i) 'Ted often acts like a nitwit,' said Ian. 'You could think he was a real bonehead if you didn't know him.'
(j) 'Ugh! I hate spiders!' Karen cried.
(k) 'Good heavens! You did give me a fright, Steve,' said his mother.

2   Rewrite the story about Charlie (pages 35 and 36), changing the direct to reported speech.

3   Rewrite this passage, changing the direct to reported speech.

A Spanish student returned to his village from his first term at university, determined to show his parents how much he had learned. Among the things they were going to eat for lunch were two hard-boiled eggs on a plate.

The student stealthily took one from the plate, and said to his father, 'Papa, how many eggs are there here on this plate?'

'One,' said his father solemnly.

'And now, how many are there?' said his son, replacing the other egg.

'Two.'

'Then the two that are here on the plate now, and the one that was here before, make three. So the eggs on the plate must be three, mustn't they?'

37

His father scratched his head. The problem posed by his clever son seemed to him very difficult, and he said uncertainly, 'I suppose they must.'

His mother, a very practical woman, intervened. Taking one egg, she put it on her husband's plate and said, 'That one is for your father, the other one is for me, and you can eat the third.'

Traditional Spanish, trans. Albert Rowe

4 Give an outline of the story in no more than six lines.

5 Study the sketch, then write accurate detailed descriptions of the family.

6 In these two passages from *The Pickwick Papers*, by Charles Dickens, the stranger is Mr Jingle. Imagine that you were present while he was speaking. Rewrite the passages in complete sentences in reported speech.

(a) 'Heads, heads—take care of your heads!' cried the loquacious stranger, as they came out under the low archway, which in those days formed the entrance to the coach-yard. 'Terrible place—dangerous work—other day—five children—mother—tall lady, eating sandwiches—forgot the arch—crash—knock—children look round—mother's head off—sandwich in her hand—no mouth to put it in—head of a family off—shocking, shocking!'

(b) 'Ah! fine place,' said the stranger, 'glorious pile—frowning walls—tottering arches—dark nooks—crumbling staircases, old cathedral too—earthy smell—pilgrim's feet worn away the old steps—little Saxon doors—confessionals like money-takers' boxes at theatres—queer customers those monks—Popes, and Lord Treasurers, and all sorts of old fellows, with great red faces, and broken noses, turning up, every day—buff jerkins too—match-locks—Sarcophagus—fine place—old legends too—strange stories: capital.'

7   Turn this extract from Alan Plater's television play *Terry* into reported speech. Be sure to convey all the essential meaning of the conversation, and include the stage directions in a suitable form.

(Terry comes into the Manager's office. It is a small office, not very impressive—the same might also be said of the Manager, who is quietly harassed.)
MANAGER. What is it this time, Terry?
TERRY. I've had enough, Mr Hackenschmidt.
MANAGER. Had enough?
TERRY. That's right.
MANAGER. You can't have had enough . . . I'll never be able to find a replacement . . .

TERRY. I don't want to make a fuss, but I think I'm going out of my mind.

MANAGER. Couple of aspirins and a glass of hot milk works wonders, Terry . . .

TERRY. I'll have to have my cards.

MANAGER. It's good advice; you'll thank me for it.

TERRY. I've given Universal Products long and faithful service, Mr Hackenschmidt . . .

MANAGER. How long have you been here . . .?

TERRY. Nearly five weeks now . . .

MANAGER. Long and faithful?

TERRY. Well . . . faithful. I haven't worked anywhere else while I've been here.

MANAGER. Do you know how long I've been here, lad?

TERRY. No idea.

MANAGER. Thirty-one years.

TERRY. Yes, but are you happy?

MANAGER. Happy? Happy, what business is that of yours?

TERRY. It isn't, I just thought . . .

MANAGER. In the middle of a normal working day, you come in here asking me if I'm happy. . . . I think you'd better get out of this office before I do something desperate . . .

TERRY. Right, Mr Hackenschmidt.

Terry gives a bewildered reaction into camera, then goes out.

The manager takes two aspirins from a bottle on his desk and pours himself a glass of water. He is about to take them when Terry comes in again.

TERRY. You didn't give me my cards.

MANAGER. Here's your rotten cards! (*He throws them at him.*)

TERRY. Ta. Glass of hot milk and a couple of aspirins, is it? (*He is looking at the Manager's aspirins and glass. The Manager reacts menacingly.*) Good advice, you'll thank me for it. (*Terry makes a fast exit as the Manager hurls the glass at the door.*)

Terry pauses outside the Manager's door.

TERRY. My mam and dad, they'll be pleased as well.

8   Study the photographs, then write lively, accurate descriptions of Terry and the manager.

9   Summarise the scene in a sentence.

Literal and metaphorical language

When a word or phrase is used literally, it is used in its real or actual meaning.

When a word or phrase is applied to something it does not apply to literally to suggest a comparison, it is being used metaphorically.

The comparison is implicit (implied), not explicit (made openly).

My egg is hard-boiled.
He is very hard-boiled.

The lion roared.
The motor-bike roared away.

This food is tasteless.
What he said gave me food for thought.

The chickens are all hatched out.
Never count your chickens before they are hatched.

Dean leapt across the stream.
She leapt at the chance to come with us.

Her nose was swollen, and her face scratched.
Pat decided not to cut off her nose to spite her face.

Discussion

Which words and phrases are used in a literal and metaphorical sense in each pair of sentences?

Make up and discuss other pairs of sentences in which the same words and phrases are used literally and metaphorically.

What proverbs do you know, and what kind of language are they expressed in? What advantages have the proverbs over the explanation of their meaning?

Express in literal language the meaning of the sentences on page 42 in which words and phrases are used metaphorically, and comment on the result.

Sum up the advantages and disadvantages of metaphorical language compared with literal language. When, and for what purposes, would you take pains to use literal language?

Here are some verses on the English language to discuss. Go through the lines carefully, asking yourselves these and similar questions. What is the name of such words as are described in the first two lines? What word in verse 5 is being used both literally and metaphorically? What puns are being made or implied? What word in the last verse dates the poem, and what does the word mean?

What do you notice about the word order in many lines? Why does the author put the words in this order?

THE ENGLISH LANGUAGE

Some words have different meanings,
and yet they're spelt the same.
A cricket is an insect,
to play it—it's a game.
On every hand, in every land,
it's thoroughly agreed,
the English language to explain,
is very hard indeed.

Some people say that you're a dear,
yet dear is far from cheap.
A jumper is a thing you wear,
yet a jumper has to leap.
It's very clear, it's very queer,
and pray who is to blame
for different meanings to some words
pronounced and spelt the same?

A little journey is a trip,
a trip is when you fall.
It doesn't mean you have to dance
whene'er you hold a ball.
Now here's a thing that puzzles me:
musicians of good taste
will very often form a band—
I've one around my waist!

You spin a top, go for a spin,
or spin a yarn maybe—
yet every spin's a different spin,
as you can plainly see.
Now here's a most peculiar thing,
'twas told me as a joke—
a dumb man wouldn't speak a word,
yet seized a wheel and spoke.

A door may often be ajar
but give the door a slam,
and then your nerves receive a jar—
and then there's jars of jam.
You've heard, of course, of traffic jams,
and jams you give your thumbs.
And adders, too, one is a snake,
the other adds up sums.

A policeman is a copper,
it's a nickname (impolite!),
yet a copper in the kitchen
is an article you light.
On every hand, in every land,
it's thoroughly agreed—
the English language to explain
is very hard indeed!

Harry Hemsley

Written work

1   Write ten pairs of sentences in which you use words and phrases in both their literal and metaphorical sense.
2   Write a careful, literal description of: (a) a room you know well; (b) a scene you know well.
3   Use metaphorical language to write vivid, imaginative descriptions of the same room and scene.
4   Give a clear and orderly account of the discussion you had on the language uses in Harry Hemsley's verses.

Similes, metaphors and cliches

When one thing is explicitly compared to another to reveal their similarity, the comparison is a simile.

Jack is like a little monkey.

He is as tough as leather.

The wind was as strong as a giant.

Stephanie is weaker than water.

When one thing is said to be another, the statement is a metaphor.

Jack is a real little monkey.

Mr Bray is a very hard-boiled customer.

Stuart is a veritable lion in a fight.

She is a demon.

An expression which has been used so often that the image or idea it presents has lost most of its original meaning and impact is known as a cliche.

Cliches have their uses. In our everyday conversations, we do not stop to think whether or not the similes, metaphors and metaphorical language we use so frequently, naturally and unconsciously are cliches

45

or not. We use them because they are familiar and will instantly convey our essential meaning.

Discussion

An expression which is a cliche to one person may not be so to another. Why?

Which of the similes, metaphors and examples of metaphorical language on pages 42 and 45 do you consider to be cliches, and why?

Which of these examples of similes, metaphors and metaphorical language do you consider to be cliches, and why?

as slippery as glass; as heavy as lead; she is a chatterbox; he is a donkey; the street is choked with traffic; the engine was coughing and spluttering; he smiled warmly; she cut him dead

Here is a list of similes. Which would you use in your written work, and which would you not, and why?

as agile as a monkey; as bald as a badger; as proud as a peacock; as talkative as a magpie; as meek as a mouse; as ugly as sin; as alike as two peas; as bitter as gall; as sweet as sugar; as rich as Croesus; as sharp as a razor; as spineless as a jellyfish; as mad as a March hare; as obstinate as a mule; as pale as death; as pretty as paint; as happy as a lark; as mum as an oyster; as industrious as an ant; as lazy as a toad; as lively as a cricket; as fit as a fiddle; as grave as a judge; as green as grass; as complacent as a cat; as dead as a doornail; as honest as a mirror

In your own writing, when and for what reasons ought you to try to use similes, metaphors and metaphorical language which are fresh and original, or at least fresher than those in common use?

Are proverbs cliches? Why? When, and for what reasons, would you use them?

Written work

1 Copy the similes from the list that you decided you would use in your written work.
2 Use each simile in an interesting sentence.
3 Write down five proverbs.

4   In what kind of language are they expressed?
5   Put into your own words as clearly and simply as possible what each means.
6   Explain what has been gained and lost by putting the proverbs into your own words.

Free verse: haiku and senrȳu

A very ancient form of free verse is the Japanese haiku.

A haiku consists of three lines. The first and third lines have five syllables, while the second line has seven syllables.

A true haiku has only one subject—nature. When the Japanese used the same form of free verse to write about other things, they called the poem a senrȳu.

Here are four modern examples of haiku to read and discuss. When is language being used literally, and when metaphorically, and what do both kinds contribute to the poems?

Like an iron fist
with twisted sinews, blackthorn
writes the wind's story.
        Betty Parvin

The old tree is bare
But its roots grow menacing.
A nearby wall cracks.
        Wanda Barford

Willow-herb in wind:
Cloud skeins hurrying over,
Whole field migrating.
        John Wareham

That falling petal
Returning to the white rose
Is a butterfly.
        A. R. Ward

And here are four examples from *The Penguin Book of Japanese Verse* of senrȳu translated from the Japanese.

Now the man has a child
He knows all the names
Of the local dogs.

She suckles her baby:
'On the shelf
You'll find some sardines.

Sheltering from the rain,
The words on the notice
Are learnt off pat.

The bachelor
Gives humblest thanks
For a single stitch.

Writing and collecting haiku and senrȳu

Try writing some haiku and senrȳu. Any tiny observation, memory or experience can provide the subject-matter. Here are some moments to set you going: birth of a baby; a baby's cries; a baby's first smile; a baby's first step; a harassed mother trying to feed the baby and prepare the meal for the rest of the family; a father getting an attack of acute lumbago while gardening; a grumbling grandparent; a pupil sharpening a pencil, misbehaving, falling asleep in class, or not having a pen; a robin in winter; starlings or sparrows quarrelling; a hawk poised ready to swoop; a starving, stray dog; shire horses; a cow and calf; a traffic jam; a jet aircraft taking off or landing.

Those of you who are interested could devote some time each week to writing haiku and senrȳu. The best could be collected and displayed from time to time on a noticeboard, or put into an anthology.

The poems could be typed, or artistically written or lettered by hand, and illustrated.

Making sure: verse, rhyme, metre and rhythm

'Obituary'

Life's little day is fading fast; upon the mountain's brow, the sinking sun is gleaming red: the shadows lengthen now. The twilight hush comes on apace, and soon the evening star will light us to those chambers dim where dreamless sleepers are; and when the curfew bell has rung that calls us all to rest, and we have left all earthly things at Azrael's request, O may some truthful mourner rise and say of you or me: 'Gee-Whiz! I'm sorry that he's dead: he was a honey-bee!'

Walt Mason

'A Fact'

I bought a chicken in the street and hung it up to serve as meat; but
when I came to view the bird, 'twas black and green and looked absurd.
Was I despondent? Never—no—your Wilhelmina's never so, though I
had lost my lunch, 'twas true, and wasted five and sixpence too. I sat
me down and took a breath, thought fragrantly of Life and Death, of
Strength and Grace and Love and Power, and so I mused for half an
hour. Then up I rose, replete with calm, and softly sang the Hundredth
Psalm; I gave the chicken to my mother and sallied forth to buy
another.

Bridget Muller

Written work

1 Both 'Obituary' and 'A Fact' were written as printed above, i.e. as
  prose. Rewrite them as verse.
2 Show what the rhyme scheme is.
3 Mark the metre.

4   How many feet are there in each line?
5   Rewrite the first four lines of each piece of verse, and mark the natural speech rhythms.
6   Comment on the interplay of metre and speech rhythms in both sets of four lines.
7   Which of these pairs of words could be used as rhymes in a verse, and why? fun, tone; see, free; aching, seeking; adapted, contraption; honorary, dromedary; sweetly, greeting
8   Rewrite this verse so that it becomes a limerick:

There was an old man of Dunoon
Who always ate soup with a fork.
For he said, 'As I eat
Neither fish, fowl nor flesh,
I should otherwise finish too quick.'

9   Show that you fully understand the pattern of a limerick by making up some, using these first lines or some of your own.

A cheerful young girl in Form Four

There once was a lad called Willie

A dashing young lady from Spain

There was a young man of St Ives

Essay topics

1   My First Outing.
2   Motor Racing.
3   My Ideal Flat.
4   Farming.
5   Write a short story to illustrate one of the following sayings:
    (a) The best things in life are free.
    (b) Don't count your chickens before they are hatched.
    (c) If a thing's worth doing, it's worth doing well.
6   Japan *or* China *or* The Far East.

Unit 4

Verb, subject and object

A sentence need have only two parts, a verb and a subject. Check that you can identify the verb (or verb group), the subject group and the subject word in these sentences.

Grass grows.

Sue Jones was singing.

The little girl was eating very quickly.

A sentence may consist of three parts—verb, subject and object.
The object may be found by asking this question: who or what is the verb acting upon?

Sue Jones was singing a difficult solo.

The little girl is eating the huge ice cream very quickly.

John lifted Bill and Gary together.

The active and passive voice of the verb

In the first of each of the following pairs of sentences, the verb is active, i.e. it is used in the active voice. This means that the subject is directly responsible for performing the action.

In the second sentence of each pair, the verb is passive (used in the passive voice). This means that the subject has the action done to it.

Sue Jones was singing a difficult solo.

A difficult solo was being sung by Sue Jones.

52

The little girl is eating the huge ice cream very quickly.

The huge ice cream is being eaten very quickly by the little girl.

The woman was dragging her yelping dog along behind her.

Her yelping dog was being dragged behind her by the woman.

The teacher ordered Terry to come to the front of the class.

Terry was ordered by the teacher to come to the front of the class.

The active form of a verb is the direct, natural form. When we use it in a sentence, the reader's attention is first caught by the subject.

The passive form of a verb is the indirect form. The natural order of the words is reversed. The object is taken out of its place in the sentence, and put at the beginning as the subject, thus catching the reader's attention first.

Discussion

Identify the verb (or verb group), the subject group, the subject word, the object group and the object word in the above sentences.

When the verb was changed from the active to the passive voice, what happened to the subject and object?

Does each pair of sentences say the same thing? If so, what is the difference between them, and how is this difference achieved?

Is there also a difference in the pace and movement of the sentences? If so, which moves quicker and is more vigorous, and why?

Thoroughly discuss when, and for what purposes, you would use the active or passive form of the verb in your writing.

Now that you have written a number of essays, discuss also these and similar questions on the kind of language you should use in an essay. How colloquial (conversational) should you be? Should you always avoid such colloquialisms as 'great', 'putrid', 'fantastic', 'lousy', 'fabulous', 'nice', 'aggravate', 'livid'? Should you ever use slang? Cliches? Well-known figures of speech? Should you use contractions? (As a part of your style? Rarely? Not at all?) Should you avoid 'e.g.', 'i.e.' and 'etc.'—the last like a plague?

An essay is a personal and subjective piece of writing. Should the subject you choose make a difference to how informally you write?

Language work

1 Rewrite these sentences, changing the verb from the active to the passive voice.
   (a) The tiny girl was kicking the ball.
   (b) That old goat is eating Rita's new hat.
   (c) She will accompany him.
   (d) A warder escorted the two prisoners into the dock.
   (e) The mother fed her five children a constant supply of biscuits.
2 Rewrite these sentences, changing the verb from passive to active.
   (a) The sack race was won by Kishan.
   (b) Every piece was picked up by us.
   (c) Each of the walls had to be painted a different colour by them.
3 Go through the sentences you have written for Nos 1 and 2.
   (a) Underline each verb or verb group;
   (b) ring each subject group;
   (c) tick each subject word.
4 Write sentences listing:
   (a) the nouns that have been used in Nos 1 and 2;
   (b) the pronouns;
   (c) the adjectives;
   (d) the prepositions.
5 Which noun has been used in the possessive singular, and what kind of noun is it?
6 Write sentences in which you correctly use the possessive plural of these nouns: hat, prisoner, mother, children.

The value of making a précis and detailed hints on how to make it

A précis is a summary of a passage written in clear, orderly prose.

To make a satisfactory précis, we have to turn one passage of prose into another and much shorter passage of prose, usually about one-

54

third the length of the original, without losing any of the essential meaning. To do this, we must obviously write the précis chiefly in our own words, though we can use some of the original words as well.

Regular practice in making a précis has the same general value as answering comprehension questions (see pp. 23 and 24).

i. It tests our understanding of language, because it is impossible to make a précis unless we first thoroughly understand the passage.

ii. It helps us improve our general command of language, because we have to express the essential meaning of the passage clearly and logically, chiefly in our own words.

iii. It accustoms us to close and careful study of a written passage, something which will stand us in good stead now and in the future.

Discuss these detailed hints on how to make a précis. Some of them will be familiar, others will be new.

1 Read the instructions carefully.

2 Read the passage quickly to get the general sense.

3 Read the passage very carefully, rereading those sections you do not fully understand.

4 Make a note of what the main theme is, i.e. what the passage is chiefly about. What you have written should be a suitable title to the passage, or form the basis of one.

5 Keep your title constantly in mind while you work on your précis—the précis must be built around it.

6 Work from the passage. Jot down, in note form, the important points that you intend to include in your précis. Leave a space between each point and the next (see No. 7 below).

7 Check whether there are any modifying or supporting points to be added to the main points.

8 Make in your own words a prose draft of the précis from your notes.

9 Cut the draft to the required number of words, making sure not to omit any of the essential meaning.

10 Make a neat fair copy of the final version.

The written work that follows covers some of the techniques that will help you make a satisfactory précis. Thoroughly discuss the techniques involved before you write your answers.

(You need not necessarily do all the questions at one sitting. You can do some now, and others from time to time later, as your teacher advises.)

1 Rewrite these sentences, substituting a brief general term for each
   detailed list.
   (a) He brought with him one of the new double-bladed safety
   razors, a large tube of shaving cream, soap, flannel, toothbrush
   and paste, comb, hairbrush and a large towel.
   (b) I will need a sweater, shirt, shorts, socks, towel, half-a-dozen
   balls and my tennis racquet.
   (c) The cupboard was crammed with bowls, frying pans,
   saucepans, casseroles, cake tins, whisks, mincers, wooden spoons,
   metal ladles, knives of all sizes and an enormous fish slice.
   (d) The garden contained rows and rows of cabbages, carrots,
   onions, broad beans, runner beans, peas and potatoes.
   (e) The inhabitants of London, Paris, Brussels, Rotterdam and
   Rome have to put up with engines roaring, gears clashing, brakes
   screeching, and tyres screaming from the moment they wake up to
   the time they fall asleep.
   (f) As you pass along this quay, the air is pungent with tobacco,
   then it overpowers you with the fumes of rum, then you are nearly
   sickened with the stench of hides and huge bins of horns. Shortly
   afterwards, the atmosphere is fragrant with coffee and spice. Here
   you sniff the fumes of the wine, and there the peculiar fungus-
   smell of dry rot.

2 Shorten this passage by cutting out adjectives, adverbs and
   repetitions of words, e.g. some nouns and conjunctions.

   Black saloons and yellow saloons, bright red sports cars and
   battered grey vans, green buses and blue buses, tiny two-seaters
   and gigantic Mercedes and Rolls—all poured slowly along the
   hot roads towards the race-track. There already the enormous
   park was crammed full to overflowing and the sunlight sparkled
   and winked on windscreen glass and bright paint and polished
   chrome.

3 Shorten this passage by using the active instead of the passive
   voice of the verb.

The wagon train was being attacked by a horde of savage Indians. Muzzle-loading rifles were being fired as rapidly as possible by the besieged, and showers of deadly arrows from the yelling redskins were being sent whizzing and humming into the closed circle of the covered wagons.

4   Rewrite the passage, shortening it further by applying the technique used in No. 2.

5   Shorten this passage by applying the same techniques as you did in Nos 3 and 4. Use no more than forty words.

The cricket ball was hit a tremendous way by the captain, a big burly fellow who seemed to rely more on good luck than any of the recognised batting skills. The bat had been lifted for the stroke as if it were a golf club, not a cricket bat. It had then been viciously swung at the poor ball in a wide circle, with truly formidable power. The sharp sound of the stroke, echoing like a rifle shot, had been heard by a group of people, lazing in the sun far away by the river, and an old man deep asleep in front of the pavilion had been startled wide awake by the unexpected noise.

6   Shorten these passages by turning the direct into indirect speech, and by any of the other techniques practised so far.

(a) Mr S. F. James opened his talk with these words: 'I am very delighted indeed to be invited here to address you on a subject that is very dear to my heart, namely, the proper use of leisure.' Just at that moment, an enormous man stood up in the audience and shouted in a very loud voice, 'That's all very well, guv, but I ain't got no bloomin' leisure!'

(b) He wrote, 'The ice in the pond at length begins to be honeycombed, and I can set my heel in it as I walk. Fogs and rains and warmer suns are gradually melting the snow; the days have grown appreciably longer; and I see how I shall get through the winter without adding to my woodpile, for large fires are no longer necessary. I am on the alert for the first signs of spring, to hear the chance note of some arriving bird, or the striped squirrel's chirp, for his stores must be now nearly exhausted, or see the woodchuck venture out of his winter quarters.'

(c) The meeting, like all staff meetings, was a very lengthy one.
As usual, the headmaster spoke first. 'I'm very sorry indeed to
have to call you together without notice like this,' he said, 'but this
is an emergency.' He cleared his throat and then went on, 'This
morning a group of boys—fifteen in number, so I've been reliably
informed—deliberately defied the deputy head by getting up and
walking out of his room after they had been told to remain where
they were.'

At this point one of the young masters, the one who had only
joined the staff last term, got on his feet and said in an irritated
voice that trembled as he spoke, 'But surely, Headmaster, you can
hardly blame the boys for that, now, can you?'

It seemed for a moment that the headmaster would fall down in
sheer amazement. He staggered back, and his face turned a
violent red. Then he cried, 'Really, Mr Smith, do you know, sir,
what you're saying?'

7 Shorten each of the following passages, using the techniques
already practised, then make it into one sentence by using an
appropriate conjunction (suggested conjunctions are added in
brackets).

(a) We were operating in a huge game reserve. It was quite usual
to come out of our four-man tent in the chill of the early morning,
and find herds of zebras, gazelles, buffaloes and ostriches grazing
around us. We could also see many rhinos, and a lot of
particularly unpleasant snakes. (*and*; *also*)

(b)   Most disturbing of all was the incredible way in which
fully-grown lions roamed about us at night. So careless and
clumsy were they that they often fell over our tightly-stretched
tent ropes. This annoyed them terribly. They coughed and
spluttered with rage, so much so that they were the chief ones that
kept us from having a good night's sleep. (*and*)

(c)   The migration of animals has been observed by man for
thousands of years, and it is still one of the most fascinating
questions in nature. We cannot be sure that all the incredible facts
we have now gathered about this phenomenon provide us with a
full explanation of it. (*though*)

(d)   Invention is seldom, as so many people imagine, a matter of
spontaneous creation, but rather of evolution. No inventor has
ever thought of anything entirely original. Even such
fundamental and classical inventions as the wheel, the first tool,
or the first power-driven machine were improvements or
adaptations of things already in existence rather than brand-new
discoveries. (*because*)

(e)   A thief broke into the house of a holy man, but after the most
diligent search had the mortification of finding nothing. The good
man, discovering what had happened, took the blanket on which
he had been sleeping and laid it in the path of the thief, so that he
might not be disappointed. (*so; as*)

8   Summarise this passage in one sentence. Begin with 'Because' or 'As a result of', and use 'though' to link the contents of the first to the second paragraph.

We have found out a great deal about migratory routes, and when they take place. In 1899 the first scientific ringing of birds was made, and this has been going on ever since. In Great Britain alone nearly 3 000 000 birds have been ringed since that time, and over 30 000 000 in the world as a whole. Of these, over 1 000 000 have been recovered.

Today there are more ways than ever of finding out about migration. We watch, trap and study them in over 300 permanent observation stations scattered about the globe; we track them—even the smallest—by radar at a range of 80 miles; we sight them as they fly across the moon; and at night we listen to them with sensitive microphones.

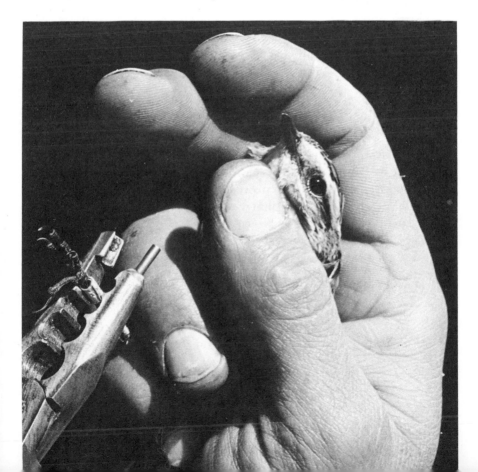

9   Summarise this passage in one sentence. Begin with 'Viewing has displaced listening, for', and use 'although' as your second conjunction.

The displacement of listening by viewing is natural enough. At times when it is possible to 'sit around' it is, other things being equal, more fun to see and hear than just to hear. Viewing is, in short, commonly regarded as 'much better than listening'. But our national leisure-time budget would also show that the time devoted to viewing is not wholly accounted for by the time taken from listening.

Making and writing-up notes

1   Look these up in an encyclopedia, and make notes of the most interesting points:
(a) Cricket
(b) Your favourite game
(c) Big game hunting
(d) Bird migration
2   Use your notes to write clear prose accounts of what you have found out.

Writing a description and telling a story

1   Take hints from No. 2 on page 56, and describe the scene before the beginning of any two of these: a football match, or any other sporting event; a fair; a protest march; a school outing.
2   Write a detailed, imaginative description of the cricketer mentioned in No. 5 on page 57.
3   Tell an amusing story based on the same extract.
4   Reread extract 6 (b) on page 58, then write a lively prose description of the coming of any of the seasons.
5   Tell an imaginary story based on the extract quoted in No. 6 (c) on page 59.
6   Describe and comment upon a film or book in which some of the animals mentioned in No. 7 (a) and (b) on pages 59 and 60 played a part.

The rule for spelling a word with ie or ei

I comes before *e*, except after *c*, when the sound rhymes with *bee*.

Exceptions: forfeit, counterfeit, seize, weir, weird.

You may find it easier to remember the rule in verse form:

When the sound is *ee*, as in *feet* or *bee*,
I comes before *e* except after *c*.
There are five exceptions, as I very much feared:
Forfeit, counterfeit,
Seize, weir and weird.

Spellings and vocabulary

1   Use these words, correctly spelled, in interesting sentences:
    achieve, mischief, retrieve, chief, believe, thief, relief.
2   Write these verbs, and opposite each its noun form: believe,
    thieve, retrieve, relieve, achieve.
3   Use the nouns, correctly spelled, in interesting sentences.
4   Use these exceptions to the rule in interesting sentences, taking
    particular care to spell them correctly: seize, counterfeit, weir,
    weird, forfeit.
5   Use these words correctly spelled in interesting sentences: ceiling,
    deceive, receive, conceive, perceive.
6   Write these verbs, and opposite each its noun form: deceive,
    conceive, receive.
7   Use the nouns, correctly spelled, in interesting sentences.
8   Use these words, correctly spelled, in interesting sentences: beige,
    deign, feign, feint, freight, heinous, inveigle, skein, their.
9   The words on the following page have been used in Units 3 and 4.
    (a) Take the words one column at a time, and test with your
    neighbour that you can spell them correctly.
    (b) Learn those you misspelled, and test yourselves again.
    (c) Enter those you find difficult in your notebook for future
    learning.

I	II	III	IV
haiku	senrȳu	harassed	artistically
efficiently	summary	casserole	Mercedes
chrome	burly	viciously	formidable
pavilion	leisure	gradually	emergency
defied	gazelles	buffaloes	ostriches
incredible	phenomenon	mortification	disappointed
migratory	practised	camouflage	radiator
heights	multiplicity	received	achievements

10 Use these words, correctly spelled, in sentences which will clearly illustrate their meaning: haiku and senrȳu, harassed, burly, formidable, phenomenon, mortification, migratory, camouflage, multiplicity, received, achievements.

Making sure: using the full stop, question mark, exclamation mark and comma to separate one unit of meaning from another

To make our meaning clear when we are writing, we must:
i. use the appropriate words in the appropriate order to express our meaning;
ii. punctuate those words so that their meaning is completely clear.

We can divide punctuation marks into four groups according to their use. Here we will deal with the first group.

The first group of punctuation marks is used to separate one unit of meaning—sentence, clause, phrase or word—from another. The punctuation marks used for this purpose are the full stop, the question mark, the exclamation mark and the separating comma.

(a) The full stop (.)

A full stop separates one complete statement, instruction, mild command or indirect question from what follows.

Jugdev is coming home today.

He was told to paint the door next.

Put the typewriter on the table.

Mother asked Kim where she had been.

(b) The question mark (?)

A question mark separates a direct question from what follows. A direct question is a question that needs an answer.

Where has Kim been?

What colour is your new dress?

Do you know what the time is?

(c) The exclamation mark (!)

An exclamation mark separates exclamatory sentences and words expressing sudden strong feeling from what follows.
   An exclamation mark is also used to end a forceful instruction or command.

What a lovely day it is!

Listen! I can hear someone coming.

Ah! so there you are at last.

Keep your head down!

Cut it along this line, not that!

(d) The separating comma (,)

   i. A comma is used to separate simple items in a list, including items in dates, addresses, and so on.

In the farmyard, Prakash saw a horse, two cows, two donkeys, a goat and its kid, five turkeys, three geese and more hens than he could count.

It happened on 2 April, 1763.

Andrew M. V. Clarke, 14 St Thomas's Road, Basingstoke, Hampshire.

The book is *Oliver Twist*, by Charles Dickens.

ii. A comma is used to separate clauses linked by the conjunctions *and, but, or, because, so, yet, although, while.*

He offered it to me, and I took it.

Julie promised to go, but she did not.

Did you bring your camera, or did you forget it?

Leslie was sure it was Dean, because he saw his face quite plainly.

It was becoming too dark to see, so Uncle switched on the light.

The food was very tasty, yet Angela found she had no appetite.

He would keep biting his nails, although he had been told over and over again not to.

Terry laid the table, while Sally prepared the meal.

iii. A comma is used to separate an introductory word, phrase or clause from the main sentence.

Unfortunately, the car would not start.

Tom, that book is mine.

This done, we sat down and relaxed.

His armies defeated, Hitler committed suicide.

Taking his advice, she carried her raincoat and umbrella.

Having heard it once, Vinod did not want to hear it again.

If that happens, we will come at once.

When they reached the door, they found it was locked.

Although the weather was so bad, we enjoyed our holiday.

iv. A comma is used to avoid ambiguity, so making the intended meaning completely clear.

Do shoot Ned.	We are trying Brian.
Do shoot, Ned.	We are trying, Brian.

Christopher Robin has arrived.	Are you going to eat Mike?
Christopher, Robin has arrived.	Are you going to eat, Mike?

Written work

1   Write three statement sentences about the weather.
2   Write clear instructions on how to open a tin of sardines.
3   Write three mild commands you might give a young relative.
4   Write four direct questions you might ask your neighbour.
5   Turn the direct questions into indirect questions.
6   Turn these direct into indirect questions.
  (a) 'Where have you been, Leslie?' asked Father.
  (b) They said, 'Will you and your brother come as well?'
  (c) 'What time is it?' Gary said.
  (d) She gazed upwards and said, 'How high is that tree, do you think?'
7   Write an exclamatory sentence expressing sudden strong feeling at seeing:
  (a) a most beautiful sunset;
  (b) a rat emerging from a drain;
  (c) a Punch and Judy show;
  (d) an elephant;
  (e) a mother chastising her child.
8   Use four exclamatory words in correctly punctuated sentences.

9 Write correctly punctuated sentences in which you list:
   (a) six objects in your classroom;
   (b) the full names of five members of your class;
   (c) four television programmes you watched recently;
   (d) the colours of the rainbow.
10 Write two correctly punctuated sentences stating:
   (a) your date of birth and your address;
   (b) three books you have read recently, with the names of the authors and publishers.
11 Copy these sentences, correcting the punctuation.
   (a) When Tom arrived he unexpectedly brought his father with him
   (b) Unfortunately for us the car had a puncture
   (c) After waiting for an hour Raj decided her sister had forgotten their meeting
   (d) The five pigeons had settled on one side of the roof while the cat crept stealthily up the other
   (e) The two ships collided but fortunately neither was damaged very much
   (f) The job done at last mother was able to turn her attention to us
   (g) Realising it would be very difficult Diane gritted her teeth and began
   (h) If you can bring some crockery it will be most helpful
   (i) The horses were grazing peacefully and the two boys moved quietly among them
   (j) Brenda may I see your new book
   (k) He tried to mend it although he knew full well he could not
   (l) We must set out soon today because we were late yesterday

Essay topics

1 Furniture.
2 Unidentified Flying Objects (UFOs).
3 Describe an occasion when you have been in a large crowd at a public event. Concentrate on the crowd, its behaviour and

reactions, the variety of individuals in it, rather than on the event itself.

4 Keeping Up With Fashion.
5 'Differences of accent are of no importance.' Discuss.
6 Bird-watching.

Unit 5

Finite and non-finite verbs, infinitives, verbal nouns and participles

Any form of a verb that can stand on its own and make sense in a sentence is known as a finite verb. The word 'finite' has here its grammatical meaning of 'complete'.

He exercises once a week.

She ran.

They have been here for two hours.

There are two non-finite (incomplete) forms of a verb.
i. The infinitive, which is the name by which we refer to a verb, and which is written with 'to' in front of it: to go; to see; to swim; to eat.
ii. The *-ing* form of the verb: going, seeing, swimming, eating.
   Both the infinitive and the *-ing* form of the verb can function as nouns. When the *-ing* form of the verb fulfils this function, it is known as a verbal noun or gerund.

To see something is to believe it exists.

To err is human, to forgive divine.

Swimming is a healthy pastime.

Eating was his favourite occupation.

The *-ing* form of a verb is also frequently used as an adjective.

We took care not to disturb the sleeping child.

His performing dogs are all Pekinese.

Neither the infinitive nor the *-ing* form of the verb can function on its own as a verb in a sentence. *He eats,* but not *He to eat* or *He eating*; *They go,* but not *They to go* or *They going*; *They travelled all day*, but not *They to travel* or *They travelling all day*.

The *-ing* form of a verb can only function as a verb when it is completed by an auxiliary verb. When it does this, it is known as the present participle of the verb.

He is eating.

They were going home.

We had been travelling all day.

Ann will be playing on Saturday.

The *-ed* form of a verb has two functions.
i. It is used to make one of the past tenses of the verb
ii. It is used with auxiliaries to make other past tenses of the verb. When it is used in this way, it is known as the past participle of the verb.

We travelled all day.
We had travelled all day.

They waited an hour for us.
They had waited an hour for us.

We shared the task.
The task was shared by us.

Written work

1   Use these finite verbs in sentences: shouted, swims, slept, shivers, grumbled.
2   Write the infinitives of the finite verbs in No. 1.
3   Use the infinitives in sentences.

4 Use these verbal nouns in sentences: shouting, swimming, sleeping, shivering, grumbling, cutting, studying, collecting, reading, sailing.
5 Use these verbal adjectives in sentences: shouting, sleeping, shivering, grumbling, cutting, jangling, heating.
6 Use each of these past participles as part of a past tense in a sentence: shouted, travelled, shivered, shared, tired, overjoyed.

Clauses and phrases

Now that we know the difference between the finite and non-finite forms of a verb, we can understand and use new and grammatically more accurate definitions of clauses and phrases:
 i. A clause is a group of words that contains a finite verb.
 ii. A phrase is a group of words that may or may not contain an infinitive, verbal noun or participle, but does not contain a finite verb.
    Identify and discuss the clauses and phrases in these sentences.

Vicky stood quite still: Tracy began to move about restlessly.

We were on one side, and they were on the other.

Jack sang tenor, while Trevor sang bass.

Hearing his sister, he ran forward.

This said, Yashpal smiled as if he had made a really clever remark.

When the sun shines, I feel so happy that I could sing.

Suraj, her breath coming in short gasps, crept forward.

Grandfather, who is now almost ninety, is still quite sprightly.

The present which you gave me has been broken.

Written work

I Write the clauses from the above examples which could be used as sentences exactly as they stand.

2   Write the clauses which could not be used as sentences exactly as
    they stand.
3   What would have to be missed out from each of the clauses in the
    second example to enable them to be used as sentences?
4   Write the phrases from the example sentences on page 72.
5   Use the phrases in sentences of your own.
6   Write the clauses from page 66, ii., which could not be used as
    sentences exactly as they stand.
7   Rewrite them so that they are now complete sentences.
8   Write the phrases in the sentences on pages 66–7, iii.
9   Use the phrases in correctly punctuated sentences of your own.
10 Rewrite the last three sentences on pages 66–7, iii., substituting
    clauses of your own for the second clause in each sentence.

'Mr Prodhurst and The Gladiator'

*Mr Prodhurst is seventy-eight. He is standing at the double gates of his scrapyard,
when Joe passes.*

'Hello, lad,' said Mr Prodhurst. 'Are you in a hurry?'
    'No, not really,' said Joe. 'Did you want something?'
    'I wonder, lad, if you'd run to the chemist for me and get me a bottle?
It's me leg, you see. It's given out, and the bottle's for me chest.' He
coughed and the sound came as a deep, painful jangling, as if there were
lots of things loose inside Mr Prodhurst. 'Will you do it for me?'
    'Aye. What is it you want?'
    'It's on this bit of paper. There's the money; it'll be three-and-
sixpence.'
    'I might have to wait,' said Joe; 'I'd go indoors if I were you. I'll fetch
it in to you.'
    'Will you, lad? That's kind of you. All right, I'll go on in. I'll leave the
gate open. Just come through the yard; you'll see the light through the
window.'
    'All right,' said Joe. 'I won't be a tick.'
    He was back within five minutes, and when he pushed the gate open
and went into the yard he thought, Eeh! it looks just like Steptoe's yard.

73

In the light from the window he picked his way around a jumble of old iron, then knocked at the door.

'Come in, come in,' Mr Prodhurst cried, and Joe went in, only to stop dead within the doorway. Eeh! as he said to himself later, he had never seen anything like it, even on the telly. Steptoe's room was a palace to this. There was no shade on the electric bulb, and it showed up an old iron bed standing in one corner of the room, a square wooden table in the middle, a number of chairs, a chest of drawers and a conglomeration of boxes of all shapes and sizes lining the walls. It wasn't until he stood near the table and handed the old man his medicine and his change that he noticed that the boxes were full of books. The up-sided boxes held ordered rows of books, but the ones standing on their bottoms looked as if the books had just been thrown into them. Yet in spite of the jumble, the place looked sort of bare, and clean.

'You . . . you lookin' at my library?' Mr Prodhurst turned his unshaven face towards the wall behind him. 'I like books. Always read books. All my life I've read books. Do you read?'

'Well, some kinds of books, technical books,' said Joe.

'You live by yourself?' said Joe.

'No, not entirely, lad. I have The Gladiator. I'll never be alone as long as I've got him.'

'The . . . the Gladiator?' Joe screwed up his face.

'Me horse.'

'Oh, your horse.' Joe's head was back, his mouth wide and his eyes bright. 'I've never heard a horse called The Gladiator. Gladiators were Romans.'

'Aye, they were that, lad, and they were called gladiators because they were brave. And my horse is a brave horse, a fine horse, and so I named him The Gladiator. Listen, that's him. He knows I'm talkin' about him. Oh, he knows.'

There was a neighing sound from beyond the wall, and Joe looked towards the fireplace and the old man said, 'His stable's just t'other side. I don't need to go outside, I had a door put in from the room. Come and have a look.'

Joe got up and followed the old man. The process was very slow, because Mr Prodhurst sort of dragged one leg after him.

They went through the door in the corner of the room, Mr Prodhurst switched the light on, and there, opposite to them, lying on a big pile of clean straw, was the oldest-looking horse Joe had ever seen in his life.

'Aren't you going to get up and say hello?' Mr Prodhurst was talking as if to another person and the horse responded as if he was a person, for, struggling slowly to his feet, he stood up and came towards the old man and Joe.

The Gladiator was a big horse, and Joe had the impression of bones sticking out of him at all angles from his body. When the animal put his head down to Joe and pushed him gently in the chest, Joe almost fell over backwards, and not a little with fright.

'He likes you, he's taken to you; he doesn't do that with everybody. Oh yes, he likes you. He's choosy, is The Gladiator.'

Mr Prodhurst now moved towards the manger and, looking down at it, said, 'You didn't make much of your tea, did you?' Then turning to Joe he added, 'His appetite isn't what it used to be. He doesn't get much exercise now and when you don't get exercise your appetite's likely to suffer. Horses and men, we're all alike. I used to take him up on to the common every Sunday. Oh, he did enjoy that, he looked forward to it. But what with me leg and one thing and another it's been impossible lately. Still, he does well enough, don't you?'

The horse now placed his muzzle against the side of Mr Prodhurst's head and the way he moved it was for all the world, Joe thought, as if he were saying, 'Yes, I do well enough.'

'Go on back to bed with you.'

Joe's eyes widened as the horse turned about, went to the corner and slowly lowered itself down on to the straw again.

When they were back in the room, Mr Prodhurst said, 'There, what do you think of him?'

Joe daren't say what he thought, except that it was wonderful the way the horse knew what was being said to him.

From *Joe and The Gladiator*, by Catherine Cookson

Discussion

Talk about the passage, and say with your reasons whether or not you enjoyed it. Judging from the extract, would you like to read the whole story? Why?

The conversation between Mr Prodhurst and Joe is a model of its kind. Study it, and make sure that you understand the rules for setting out and punctuating a passage of conversation in a story.

What can you learn from the way the rest of the passage is punctuated?

What do you notice about the way Catherine Cookson paragraphs her story? Why did she paragraph her story in this way?

Concentrate next on the method the writer adopts to build up the picture of Mr Prodhurst, Joe and The Gladiator. What physical details does she present to us? Does she present them all in one place, or dotted here and there through the narrative? What does the fact that she gives us comparatively few details allow us to do?

Compare her method with those of Dylan Thomas, Charles Dickens and Spike Milligan (pp. 9–11).

Short though the extract is, Catherine Cookson manages to reveal a great deal about the characters of Joe and Mr Prodhurst, and about what kind of a horse The Gladiator is. Put forward your reasons for agreeing or disagreeing with this statement, paying particular attention to the dialogue. Sum up what was revealed about them.

What non-finite verbs have been used in the passage, and in what form?

Descriptive and imaginative writing

1   Write lively, detailed descriptions of Joe and Mr Prodhurst which would fit what we are told about them in the extract.

2   Write a detailed description of The Gladiator, using the facts in the extracts as a basis.

3   You find yourself in a similar situation to Joe's. The scrap-merchant you do the errand for is, however, very different from Mr Prodhurst, and so are his yard, room, stable and his relationship with his horse. Taking hints from the extract, describe the scene, and give an account of what happened that will reveal as much as possible of the character of yourself, the scrap-merchant, and the horse. (Be sure to include some dialogue.)

4   Imagine that Mr Prodhurst asks Joe to take The Gladiator to the common next Sunday to give him some exercise. Joe agrees. All goes well at first, but then. . . . Tell the story, beginning when Joe arrives at the scrapyard to collect The Gladiator.

5   Make up a story about someone taking a pet for a walk, with disastrous consequences. Begin by describing the owner and the pet, and reveal enough of their characters to give the reader an inkling of what is going to happen in the story.

6   Write detailed descriptions of the appearance, temperament and habits of two animals you know well.

7   You have been given the pet you have always wanted. Write a letter to a friend describing it, and your feelings when you got it.

8   Draw and correctly address the envelope.

Vocabulary, comprehension and précis

The greater our vocabulary, the greater our power to comprehend what we read. The hints on making a précis (pp. 54 and 55), and on doing comprehension questions (pp. 23 and 24), stress that understanding a passage is of primary importance to both. They also remind us that we can often deduce the meaning of an unfamiliar word from its context.

We know that most words have a general meaning, but different shades of meaning depending on the context in which they are used. To ascertain which shade of meaning a word is carrying in a passage, we must study its context with care.

A knowledge of the various shades of meaning a word possesses will also enable us to express our thoughts and meanings more precisely and adequately in all our speaking and writing, in school and out.

Discussion

How would you define a person's vocabulary?

What is a synonym? How does having a good stock of synonyms, as well as knowing the various shades of meaning a word has, help us to express our thoughts and feelings more precisely and adequately?

What do you notice about the first three hints for answering comprehension questions (p. 23), and the first four hints for making a précis (p. 54)?

Put into your own words the connection between comprehension and précis.

What part does the ability to make quick, brief notes play in making a précis?

Exercises in comprehension and précis

A   Camouflage is practised by animals of very different types. Creatures that are protectively coloured or patterned harmonise with their surroundings and are invisible. To do this they must adjust themselves to those surroundings, either by remaining motionless or by some other suitable behaviour. One outstanding example is the kudu.

Of all the African antelopes, there is none of so fine appearance as the great kudu bull. Standing as much as four-and-a-half feet from ground to shoulders, its stillness in the face of danger, and its light brown colour with five or six stripes down the sides, are perfect camouflage. The large horns, in a corkscrew spiral, may measure up to fifty-one inches, and are the longest known in the animal kingdom.

1   What is camouflage?
2   What synonyms could be substituted for these in the sentences in which they occur: practised, harmonise, invisible, motionless?
3   Use the words themselves in sentences which clearly illustrate their meaning.
4   What are the antonyms of: invisible, motionless, suitable?
5   Use the antonyms in sentences to demonstrate their meaning.
6   Explain with examples how these harmonise with their surroundings: (a) creatures that are protectively coloured; (b) creatures that can change their colour.
7   What kind of an animal is a kudu?
8   What is the kudu an outstanding example of, and what makes it so?
9   Use a diagram to help you to explain exactly what a corkscrew spiral is.
10   Give the passage a title which will sum up its main theme.
11   Make a précis of the passage in no more than five lines.

B   We were so bitterly cold at night that we were only too glad to set off the moment it was light enough to travel (about six o'clock), and by three in the afternoon we usually stopped, not only because we were too exhausted to continue, but so that we could rest before it became too cold to sleep. As soon as we stopped, we made a leaf shelter for the night. We quickly became adept at this. We used to make a low framework with a sloping roof and lash it firmly in place with vines; then collecting the largest leaves we could find, we thatched them into the framework of the roof. We then made a huge pile of branches and leaves as a mattress, put on all our clothes, and covered ourselves with our ground sheets.

1 Why were they always glad to set off?
2 How did they travel, and for what time each day?
3 Why did they stop?
4 What synonym could be substituted for 'adept'?
5 Use 'adept' in a sentence to demonstrate its meaning.
6 When and why did they put on all their clothes?
7 Where is it likely the journey was taking place? (Give reasons for your answer.)
8 Give the passage a title which will sum up its main theme.
9 Make a précis one-third the length of the passage.

C   The source of our bodily heat is almost entirely in the foods we eat, and in the substances made from them. Every liberation of energy through the 'combustion' of these substances is accompanied by heat. Were we not provided with some cooling 'radiator' system, our body-heat would go on rising to fatal heights.

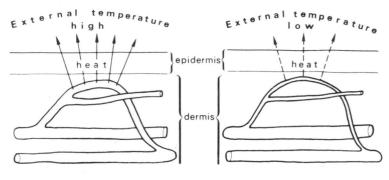

superficial blood vessels dilate —
more heat radiated out from blood
into surrounding atmosphere —
body cooled

superficial blood vessels constrict —
less radiation of heat into atmosphere —
heat conserved in deeper parts of body

The skin acts as such a radiator, but in no mere mechanical, undifferentiating way. Running through the skin are a multiplicity of little blood-vessels, capable of being stretched and contracted according to the messages received from regulating nervous centres of whose functionings we are quite unconscious. When, as during active exercise, more than normal heat is being produced within us, the skin blood-vessels swell, thus exposing a greater column of the circulating blood to the cooling influence of the air. In cold weather, especially when we are at rest, a reverse process takes place, these adaptations being finely adjusted to balance every degree of heat production.

1   What synonyms could be substituted for these words in their contexts: source, entirely, liberation, combustion, fatal, multiplicity, functionings, unconscious, reverse, adaptations, adjusted?

2   Use the words themselves in sentences to illustrate their meaning.

3 What are the antonyms of: entirely, liberation, unconscious, adjusted?
4 Use the antonyms in sentences to demonstrate their meaning.
5 Explain clearly why 'combustion' and 'radiator' are in quotation marks.
6 What is the radiator of the body?
7 What are the similarities and differences between the radiator of a car and the radiator of the body?
8 Explain in your own words how the body's radiator works.
9 Give the passage a title which will sum up what it is about.
10 Summarise the passage in good continuous prose in not more than fifty-five words.

D To the early Victorians, Michael Faraday was at one and the same time a miracle man and a source of amusement. Everyone recognised that upon him had fallen the mantle of his master, Humphry Davy. Undoubtedly Faraday was the greatest scientist of his age. All Britain was indeed proud of his achievements. The hard-headed businessmen and politicians of that period were never able to understand how a person with such a brain could be, from their point of view, so lacking in business ability. Why did he refuse to turn his mind to industrial matters, to assist them in consolidating Britain's trade supremacy and her international prestige, to speed up prosperity and to make his own fortune in the bargain? Why, in particular, did he in the age of steam fritter his energies away, year after year after year, on a mere toy like electricity?

1 Explain the phrase 'early Victorians'.
2 Why did the early Victorians think Michael Faraday was a miracle man?
3 Why did they also think he was a source of amusement?
4 Use the phrase 'source of amusement' in a sentence which will clearly illustrate its meaning.
5 (a) Who was Michael Faraday's master?
   (b) What does this word, 'master', mean in its context?

Michael Faraday   Sir Humphry Davy

6   What is meant by saying that the mantle of his master had fallen on Faraday?

7   (a) Explain fully the meaning of 'hard-headed' in its context.
(b) What part of speech is it and is it used literally or metaphorically?
(c) Use it in a sentence to demonstrate the meaning it has in its original sentence.

8   What synonyms could be substituted for these words in their context: assist, consolidating, supremacy, prestige?

9   Use the words themselves in sentences that will clearly demonstrate their meaning.

10   How could Faraday have helped the businessmen?

11   What did he prefer to do instead?

12   What did the businessmen think of electricity, and why?

13   Use the phrase, 'fritter away his energies' in a sentence that will clearly show what it means.

14   Give the passage a suitable title.

15   Make a prose summary of the passage in not more than fifty words.

Making and writing-up notes; story-telling and descriptions

1   Look up these, and make notes of some important and interesting facts: camouflage, skin, the circulatory system, Humphry Davy, Michael Faraday.
2   Use your notes to write clear, factual accounts of your findings.
3   Reread extract B on page 80, then go on with the story; or write a story of your own in which the travellers suffered great hardship.
4   Study the pictures of Michael Faraday and Humphry Davy on page 84 and then write lively, detailed descriptions of them.
5   Study the photographs of two other famous people, e.g. scientists, explorers, historians or authors, and write similar descriptions of them.

Essay topics

1   Modern Houses.
2   A Cycle Ride.
3   Saturday Night—and Sunday Morning.
4   Music.
5   'Religion has no relevance to modern life.' Discuss.
6   My Ideal Education.

Unit 6

Making a poem

The word 'making' is more appropriate than 'writing' to describe a poet's work. This is because poets do not just write their poems, but make a number of drafts until they have found the exact words they need.

LINOLEUM CHOCOLATE

Two girls running,
running laughing,
laughing lugging,
two rolls of linoleum
along London Road—
a bar of chocolate
flies from the pocket
of the second, and a man
picks it up for her, she takes it
and is about to pocket it
but then unwraps it
and the girls have a bite
to recruit the strength
of their giggling progress.

Edwin Morgan

Discussion

Read the poem carefully, then express your reasoned opinion of it, backing up what you say by quotations from the text.

Read the poem aloud a number of times. Emphasise the natural speech rhythms, and the separation made by the punctuation marks of one unit of sense from another. (Why should you also make a slight pause at the end of each line, even though there is no punctuation mark?)

In what ways do the rhythms emphasise and enrich the sense of the words?

Identify the rhymes. Do they fit into a rhyme scheme, or are they irregular? What do they and the alliteration contribute to the poem?

BLUE TOBOGGANS

scarves for the apaches
wet gloves for snowballs
whoops for white clouds
and blue toboggans

stamping for a tingle
lamps for four o'clock
steamed glass for buses
and blue toboggans

tuning forks for Wenceslas
white fogs for Prestwick
mince pies for the Eventides
and blue toboggans

TV for the lonely
a long haul for heaven
a shilling for the gas
and blue toboggans

Edwin Morgan

Discussion

Which gave you most pleasure, this poem or the other, and why?

One of the differences between this poem and the other is that this is a metrical poem. Show that this is true by reading it aloud and tapping

87

out the metre, emphasising the strong stresses. How many feet does each line contain?

Read it aloud again, emphasising the speech rhythms. Comment on the play between them and the metre.

What other differences are there between the two poems? (Consider the way the lines are organised, the refrain, the punctuation and the subject-matter.)

What similarity, if any, is there between the way Edwin Morgan made this poem and the way 'found' poems are put together? Is there, for example, any logical connection between one line and another?

How can we tell that a painting is a surrealist one? In what ways, if any, does 'Blue Toboggans' resemble a surrealist painting?

Making and collecting individual and group poems

Take hints from 'Linoleum Chocolate', and try to make some similar poems. Here is a suggested method.

i. Rough out a prose account of the subject-matter—a tiny incident you observed, or in which you took part.

ii. Use your imagination, if necessary, to reshape the subject-matter to make it more suitable for your poem.

iii. Try dividing the prose into lines of various lengths, and decide which lengths best reflect, reinforce or enrich the sense.

iv. Concentrate next upon the words and their order in the line. Try to find words which will convey the incident more clearly, freshly and vividly to the reader, and experiment with their order.

v. Poetry is made with words. This means that in finding the right words, you should bear in mind that their sound and movement is an important part of their value in a poem.

vi. You may be able to add to the pleasure the poem will give by including some alliteration and irregular rhymes. Beware, though, of using both, unless you can make it appear that they have happened naturally. Only an experienced and skilful poet can use rhyme, particularly in a rhyme scheme, successfully.

vii. Make a neat fair copy of your final draft.

Because such poems are similar to 'found' poems and surrealist pictures, you can, if you wish, make them with a friend, or in a small group. Here is a suggested method, using 'Blue Toboggans' as a model.

i. Decide on a general subject, then suggest lines having some connection with it, however vague, but not a logical connection.
ii. Play around with the order of the lines until you find the order that you like best.
iii. Arrange the lines in stanzas of two, four or six lines.
iv. Concentrate next upon the words, their sound, movement and order as before.
v. Read the lines aloud, emphasising the speech rhythms. As 'Blue Toboggans' is a metrical poem, try, if possible, to fit the speech rhythms into a metrical pattern. All the lines could contain two, three or four feet each, or particular lines in each stanza could contain the same number of feet, e.g. lines 1 and 3, two feet, lines 2 and 4, three feet, and so on.

If you find you cannot do this while at the same time keeping what appear to be the spontaneous speech rhythms, as Edwin Morgan does, then leave well alone and do not spoil your poem by forcing it into a metrical straitjacket.
vi. Make a fair copy of your final draft.

Those interested could set aside a time each week to make poems. The best could be added to your collection of haiku and senryu.

As well as making poems like 'Linoleum Chocolate' and 'Blue Toboggans', try taking lines from these and your own poems and turning them into haiku and senryu.

Unintentional ambiguity: word order and wrongly-linked participles

Ambiguity, sometimes comic in its implication, can be caused by being careless over our word order in a sentence.

Wanted, an upright piano by a gentleman with all keys intact.

The lion was shot by the warden with a broken leg.

The flat was sold to a rich lady newly decorated.

89

Sometimes we can write ambiguous sentences because we have not checked their meaning carefully enough.

The winger should have shot himself.

Pam said she was sorry she did not report the accident to the teacher.

If your baby does not like raw milk, boil it.

One word that is often used unintentionally ambiguously is 'only'. Consider the difference its position makes to the meaning of these sentences.

Only Jim saw Ray on Wednesday.

Jim saw only Ray on Wednesday.

Jim saw Ray only on Wednesday.

Most often ambiguity is caused by the careless use of a present or past participle. Because a participle does the work of an adjective, it must be correctly linked to the noun or pronoun it describes. Here are some examples of incorrect linking.

Walking along the road, three bicycles came in view.

He was knocked down by a car running across the road.

Having reached the top of the hill, the view was magnificent.

Jogging along the lane, the sky was threatening.

Having been damaged in the stern, the captain brought his ship safely back to harbour.

Being too ripe, she threw the pear away.

Written work

1   Comment on the unintentional ambiguity of these headlines, and give a version of each which has one meaning only.

Keep free from disease by killing germs

Queer Human Remains Unidentified

CHINESE SET TO WORK

Forger tells M.P. of prison fear

General Flies Back To Front

RED TAPE WARNING!

PASSENGERS ALIGHT

OFFICIAL REPORTS DECREASED OUTPUT

Killer on day out from Jail

Government direct action against poverty

BABY SWALLOWS FLY

PLEA TO STRIKE LEADER

NEW SCHOOL HEAD SAYS FIRST CLASS WORK NOT GOOD ENOUGH

Avoid accidents through careless driving

PIG TALKS IN MARKET

Girl Hits Bull's Eye

Beautiful Children's Dresses Destroyed in Blaze

BRITISH MOTOR SHOWS SUCCESS

Nation needs more conscientious workers

Briefs exchanged

2   Rewrite these sentences, altering the word order, the wording or the punctuation to remove the ambiguity.
   (a) He was knocked down by a bicycle walking across the road.
   (b) The boy told them that he had a message to leave.
   (c) Bring me five inch nails.
   (d) Mr Frame wanted to buy thirty four year old cars.
   (e) He requested the bill to be paid in advance.
   (f) I am glad to know that the gift reached you with much satisfaction.
   (g) Entering the lounge, it was seen to be full of people.
   (h) I once shot a giraffe in my bathing costume.
   (i) Fully trained nurses are usually to be found in mental hospitals.
   (j) The manufacturers do not care how their employees live so long as they grow rich.
   (k) The proprietors reserve the right to exclude those whom they think proper.
   (l) Women drivers are more likely to hit stationary objects and other cars than men.
   (m) The shop window looked so gay coming home from work this evening.
3   Carefully explain the differences in meaning in the three sentences in which 'only' is used (p. 90).
4   Use 'only' in sentences which make clear that you are referring to:
   (a) one thing you did on Saturday;
   (b) you being the sole person who did that thing;
   (c) the thing being done by you on no other day but Saturday.

Spelling rules for adding a suffix to words ending in -y

i. When *y* is preceded by a vowel, simply add the suffix: lays, saying, annoyed, employer.
Exceptions: laid, paid, said, daily, gaily.

ii. When *y* is preceded by a consonant, change *y* to *i*, then add any suffix except *-ing*: applies, business, hurried, married, marriage, studious, trier.

Exceptions: dryness, dryish; shyness, shyer, shyest; slyness, slyer, slyest, slyly; wryness, wryly; gayness, gayer, gayest; busybody, busyness (= state of being busy).

iii. When adding *ing* to *y* preceded by a consonant, the *y* is unchanged: applying, busying, hurrying, marrying, studying, trying.

Spellings and vocabulary

1 Use these words, correctly spelled, in interesting sentences: lays, said, paying, paid, said, daily, gaily.
2 Use these words, correctly spelled, in interesting sentences: applied, applying, business, busiest, busying, hurries, hurrying, marriage, marrying, studious, studying, trier, trying, dryness, shyness, slyness.
3 These words have been used in Units 5 and 6.

I	II	III	IV
finite	infinite	participle	believe
Pekinese	auxiliary	loose	hurried
conglomeration	medicine	technical	gladiator
neighing	choosey	exercise	conscientiously
temperament	vocabulary	adequately	camouflage
harmonise	combustion	radiator	undifferentiating
column	politicians	consolidating	supremacy
linoleum	recruit	toboggan	Wenceslas

(a) Test with your neighbour that you can spell them correctly.
(b) Learn those you misspelled, and retest yourselves.
(c) Enter in your notebook those you may have future difficulty with, and revise them regularly.
4 Use these words in sentences which will clearly show their meaning: auxiliary, loose, conglomeration, medicine, technical, choosey, conscientiously, recruit.

93

Making sure: using the semicolon, colon, single dash and hyphen to link one unit of meaning with another

On pages 64–7, we dealt with the group of punctuation marks used to separate one unit of meaning from another.

The punctuation marks which we shall deal with here are used to link one unit of meaning to another. These are the semicolon, the colon, the single dash and the hyphen.

(a) The semicolon (;)

i. A semicolon links one clause to another. It is most frequently used when the writer feels that the two clauses contrast with each other, balance each other or are closely linked to each other.

She was very sad; she needed cheering up.

He is a splendid lad; you will like him.

Bryn was ill all last week; nevertheless, he came to school every day.

Linda brought Vicky with her; moreover, they had both brought their dogs.

ii. A semicolon links items in a list when they are sufficiently detailed to be subdivided by commas.

She has recently read *Nicholas Nickleby*, by Charles Dickens; *A Tale of Two Cities*, also by Charles Dickens, which she enjoyed even more; and Arnold Wesker's play, *Roots*, which a friend had recommended to her.

Jake's outfit included a brand-new hunting rifle, which had cost a fortune; a shotgun, which was very old, but which he would not be without; a very light sleeping-bag, the finest money could buy; and a copy of Robert Frost's *Complete Poems*.

(b) The colon (:)

i. A colon throws the emphasis forward from an introductory remark on to what follows.

It was just as Tim expected: Pam had taken his bike.

Jake's outfit included these indispensable items: a rifle, shotgun, sleeping-bag and Robert Frost's poems.

These were the animals I was fortunate enough to see: a spiny ant-eater, two duckbill platypuses, a wombat, a marsupial tiger-cat and large numbers of ostriches and Kangaroos.

Tarangit said: 'I'm absolutely sure it was Karen I saw yesterday.'

Judith Wright's poem 'Full Moon Rhyme' begins with this line: 'There's a hare in the moon tonight'.

He came slowly towards me: a huge man with eyes that stared madly.

ii. A colon can be used to link one clause to another without the help of a conjunction when the writer feels that the clauses contrast very strongly with each other, balance each other exactly or are very closely linked.

Mary's first baby was a boy: Susan's first baby was a girl.

Speech is silver: silence is gold.

Rosemary at once began to work: her brother sat as still as if turned to stone.

(c) The single dash (—)

A single dash dramatically throws the emphasis back from the words that follow it to the words that precede it.

A free ride all the way home—that was what he wanted.

A rifle, shotgun, sleeping-bag and a book of poems—these were the items of his outfit Jake considered indispensable.

Mark was always very generous—incredibly so.

We looked everywhere—the two scooters had disappeared.

How did you manage to lose the money—how on earth did you?

(d) The hyphen (-)

i. A hyphen links words together to form compound nouns or compound adjectives.

Sara's mother-in-law is staying with us

It was the commander-in-chief who gave the order.

She was a well-liked and good-looking woman.

Jayesh really is a very happy-go-lucky lad.

Her coat was an attractive bluey-green colour.

Ted kept popping up like a jack-in-box.

He hit the bull's-eye first time.

That was only a second-class piece of work.

We had a dust-up, but we are good friends again now.

ii. A hyphen links the parts of compound numbers from twenty-one to ninety-nine, the parts of fractions, the syllables of words, and words of necessity split into two at the end of one line of print or writing and the beginning of another.

He was thirty-two, and she was twenty-eight.

I was given two-thirds of the proceeds.

'Antediluvian' consists of six syllables: an-te-di-lu-vi-an.

We were told to concentrate attention on the antepen-
ultimate paragraph.

Written work

1   Add contrasting, balancing or closely linked clauses to these to
    form one sentence:
    (a) Tony stopped
    (b) That hat is black

(c) Here were Myra's sandwiches

(d) Yesterday he was in a very bad mood

2 Add another clause to each of these, using a semicolon and a conjunction to link them:

(a) They were very, very tired

(b) Freda had been told repeatedly not to go

(c) The weather was very threatening

(d) We knew it was time to leave

3 Write correctly punctuated sentences in which you list these items. Make the items sufficiently detailed to be subdivided by commas, and introduce them with a colon:

(a) four objects in a classroom;

(b) the members of a family;

(c) three articles you possess or would like to possess.

4 Complete these sentences, using a single dash to throw the emphasis dramatically back to the words in front of the dash.

(a) Julie

(b) It was a lion

(c) We were astounded

(d) I looked at it in disbelief

(e) The thunder roared

5 Write any five odd numbers between forty and sixty.

6 Write these in words, $\frac{3}{4}, \frac{4}{5}, \frac{7}{8}, \frac{11}{12}$.

7 Divide these words into syllables: idle, prevaricate, antiquated, unbelievable.

Essay topics

1 What is there to be said for and against advertising?

2 Camping and Caravanning.

3 Smoking.

4 Each form in a school tends to develop its own characteristics. It also tends to have its own characters: two or three people well known both to the staff and to the rest of the school. Write your impressions of your form and its characters.

5 The Office of the Future.

6 Describe some of your most unpleasant experiences.

Unit 7

Prepositional usage

Remind yourselves of what a preposition is, and its function in a sentence.

Certain verbs and adverbs take certain prepositions. This means that each must be followed by its own preposition, and no other.

Here are some examples to study and discuss.

(a) fed up *with*

She was utterly fed up with having to do homework every night.

(b) different *from*

The twins were different from each other in appearance, speech and behaviour.

She is wearing a dress very different from the one she wore yesterday.

(c) differ *from*

The twins differ from each other in almost every way.

My pen differs from yours, and yours differs from Valerie's.

(d) compare *with*

What is the use of comparing your dog with mine?

Compared with Dean's bicycle, Graham's is not up to much.

(e) contrast *with*

Contrast this necklace with that, and you will easily see which is genuine and which is fake.

(f) indifferent *to*

Michael is quite indifferent to what people say about him.

(g) deduce *from*

We can sometimes deduce the meaning of an unfamiliar word from its context.

(h) initiate *into*

It is extremely difficult to initiate a Frenchman or an American into the game of cricket.

(i) conscious *of*

The more we become conscious of our mistakes, the less likely we are to continue making them.

Melanie is always very conscious of the impression she is making.

(j) sensitive *to*

The members of that family are not at all sensitive to what their neighbours think.

(k) communicate *with*

The explorers were able to communicate with the Amazonian Indians by sign language.

They communicated with each other for many years solely by letter.

(l) comment *on*

Mr Blackstock, an artist well known in the district, was kind enough to comment on my drawings.

Most of the people who comment on sport on TV seem to think we are blind.

(m) prefer *to*

Tarlock prefers hard-boiled eggs to soft.

We preferred to stay, but Myra preferred to leave.

The preposition these two verbs take depends on their sense.

i. tired *of*

Rasham was tired of waiting, and so he left.

She was tired of her sister's bad temper, and told her so.

tired *by*

Tired out by his exertions, he was glad to sit down.

ii. agree *with*

They agreed with each other over who should clean the room.

'I agree with you that it looks much better now,' Jayesh said.

agree *on*

We found it difficult to agree on what we should do next.

The secretary said, 'We must agree on the date of the next meeting before we go.'

agree *to*

'I will never agree to your leaving home!' Father shouted angrily.

Mark agreed to come with us next Saturday.

Language work

1 Look up 'compare' and 'contrast' in your dictionary, then explain the difference in their meaning.
2 Use the two verbs with their correct prepositions in sentences which will make clear the difference in meaning.
3 Explain in your own words what each of these means in its sentence (pp. 98–9): indifferent, imitate, conscious, sensitive.
4 Write a sentence of your own which will clearly illustrate this particular meaning of each, taking care to use its correct preposition.
5 Use the other verbs and adverbs from (a) to (m) and the prepositions in sentences of your own.
6 Reread the sentences on pages 98–9 in which these words occur, and decide what work each is doing. Write the word, and say what part of speech it is. Where the word is a noun, state also what kind it is: she, utterly, night, twins, were, very, one, yesterday, way, pen, yours, what, use, dog, mine, this, genuine, Michael, people, meaning, unfamiliar, its, Frenchman, game, mistakes, continue, always, impression, is, family, their, think, Amazonian, sign, language, well known, kind, hard-boiled, leave, and, temper, told, his, glad, down, it, now, secretary, with, Saturday.

'The Search'

Baslim, an old and crippled beggar, bought a child named Thorby in the slave market of the planet Sargon, and brought him up treating him as if he were his own son. In this extract from Robert Heinlein's science fiction story, Thorby is hurrying home to deliver an important message to Baslim.

The ruins of the old amphitheatre extend around one third of the periphery of the new. A dozen holes led down into the labyrinth which has served the old slave barracks; an unlimited number of routes ran underground from these informal entrances to that part which Baslim has pre-empted as a home. Thorby and he varied their route in random fashion, and avoided being seen entering or leaving.

This time, being in a hurry, Thorby went to the nearest—and on past; there was a policeman at it. He continued as if his destination had been a tiny greengrocer's booth on the street rimming the ruins. He stopped and spoke to the proprietress. 'Howdy, Inga. Got a nice ripe melon you're going to have to throw away?'

'No melons.'

He displayed money. 'How about that big one? Half price and I won't notice the rotten spot.' He leaned closer. 'What's burning?'

Her eyes flicked toward the patrolman. 'Get lost.'

'Raid?'

'Get lost, I said.'

Thorby dropped a coin on the counter, picked up a bell-fruit and walked away, sucking the juice. He did not hurry.

A cautious reconnaissance showed him that police were staked out all through the ruins. At one entrance a group of ragged troglodytes huddled sadly under the eye of a patrolman. Baslim had estimated that at least five hundred people lived in the underground ruins. Thorby had not quite believed it, as he had rarely seen anyone else enter or heard them inside. He recognised only two faces among the prisoners.

A half-hour later and more worried every minute, Thorby located an entrance which the police did not seem to know. He scanned it for several minutes, then darted from behind a screen of weeds and was down it. Once inside he got quickly into total darkness, then moved cautiously, listening. The police were supposed to have spectacles which let them see in the dark. Thorby wasn't sure this was true, as he had always found darkness helpful in evading them. But he took no chances.

There were indeed police below; he heard two of them and saw them by hand torches they carried—if snoopies could see in the dark, these two did not seem equipped for it. They were obviously searching, stun guns drawn. But they were in strange territory, whereas Thorby was playing his home field. A specialised speleologist, he knew these corridors the way his tongue knew his teeth; he had been finding his way through them in utter blackness twice a day for years.

At the moment they had him trapped; he kept just far enough ahead to avoid their torches, skirted a hole that reached down into the next level, went beyond it, ducked into a doorway and waited.

They reached the hole, eyed the narrow ledge Thorby had taken so casually in the dark, and one of them said,

'We need a ladder.'

'Oh, we'll find stairs or a chute.' They turned back. Thorby waited, then went back and down the hole.

A few minutes later he was close to his home doorway. He looked and listened and sniffed and waited until he was certain that no one was close, then crept to the door and reached for the thumbhole in the lock. Even as he reached he knew that something was wrong.

The door was gone; there was just a hole.

He froze, straining every sense. There was an odour of strangers but it wasn't fresh and there was no sound of breathing. The only sound was a faint drip-drip in the kitchen.

Thorby decided that he just had to see. He looked behind him, saw no glimmer, reached inside for the light switch and turned it to 'dim'.

Nothing happened. He tried the switch in all positions, still no light. He went inside, avoiding something cluttering Baslim's neat living room, on into the kitchen, and reached for candles. They were not where they belonged, but his hand encountered one nearby; he found the match safe and lit the candle.

Ruin and wreckage!

Most of the damage seemed the sort that results from a search which takes no account of cost, aiming solely at speed and thoroughness. Every cupboard, every shelf had been spilled, food dumped on the floor. In the large room the mattresses had been ripped open, stuffing spilled out. But some of it looked like vandalism, unnecessary, pointless.

Thorby looked around with tears welling up and his chin quivering. But when he found, near the door, Pop's false leg, lying dead on the floor with its mechanical perfection smashed as if trampled by boots, he broke into sobs and had to put the candle down to keep from dropping it. He picked up the shattered leg, held it like a doll, sank to the floor and cradled it, rocking back and forth and moaning.

From *Citizen of the Galaxy*, by Robert A. Heinlein

Discussion

Talk about the extract, and the thoughts and feelings it roused in you.

Discuss science fiction stories and films you have read and seen.

Offer a reasoned opinion on science fiction as a literary genre (type of writing).

Make a thorough study of the way the passage is written, and the language Robert A. Heinlein uses to gain his effects.

Here are some points to discuss.

Contrast the first paragraph with the last. What is the purpose of each, and what kind of language is used to fulfil that purpose?

What do you notice in general about the paragraphs, and what can we as writers learn from this? In particular, one paragraph consists of a single sentence, and another of only three words. What is their effect, and why?

What reasons can you put forward for the writer varying the length of his sentences so much? In particular, what effect do the very short sentences have in their context?

What special effects does he achieve through his punctuation, e.g. his use of the dash and the semicolon?

Identify and comment on some of the details he deliberately selected to maintain the tension and excitement of his narrative.

Written work

1   Use your imagination to write detailed physical descriptions and character studies of Thorby and Baslim. Make as many deductions as you can from the extract, and from this quotation, remembering that it describes Thorby as he was long ago when he was offered for sale.

The old beggar Baslim the Cripple twisted his half-naked body and squinted his one eye over the edge of the block. The boy did not look like a docile house servant to Baslim; he looked a hunted animal, dirty, skinny, and bruised. Under the dirt, the boy's back showed white scar streaks, endorsements of former owners' opinions.

2   Give a detailed, imaginative account of what the place where Baslim and Thorby lived might have looked like before it was searched and wrecked.

3   Write accurate, detailed descriptions of these, and sum up what sort of persons they were:
    (a) a character from a science fiction story;
    (b) a character from a science fiction film.

4   Give a clear and orderly prose summary of:
    (a) a science fiction story you have read;
    (b) a science fiction film you have seen.

5   Express your reasoned opinion of science fiction as a literary genre.

6   Describe and comment on science fiction films you have seen.

7   Write a letter to a friend *either* recommending that she/he begins to read science fiction, giving your reasons, and whetting your friend's appetite by describing one very gripping story, *or* pouring scorn on science fiction, and illustrating what you say by describing one very poor example.

8   Draw and correctly address the envelope.

Answering comprehension questions on the extract

1   Explain what an amphitheatre and a labyrinth are.

2   What were the 'informal entrances' and why were they so described?

3   If you were told to vary your route home 'in random fashion', what would you do?

4   Put into your own words what Thorby did after buying the bell-fruit.

5   What is a troglodyte?

6   What nickname did Thorby use for the policemen?

7   What were the policemen supposed to use to see in the dark, and why was Thorby reasonably sure that the two policemen searching in the dark could not see?

8   What advantage had Thorby over the policemen?

9   Why did Thorby describe the search of Baslim's dwelling as vandalism?

10   Use these words from the passage in sentences which will clearly illustrate their meaning: amphitheatre, labyrinth, random, troglodyte, speleologist, vandalism.

Punctuating a passage

Copy this passage, correcting the punctuation and putting in the necessary capital letters:

a stuffed animal arrived in britain in 1800 from the newly discovered continent of australia it was the most outlandish animal anyone had ever seen although many strange animals and plants had already been dispatched from that continent to be named and classified the animal in question was about three-quarters of a metre long and had a dense covering of fur it also had webbed feet a broad flat tail a wide rubbery beak and a spur just above the foot at the back of each hind leg although this at first puzzled the zoologists examining it they soon decided that its purpose was to secrete poison as if this were not enough to cap it all there was a single opening under the tail.

what were the zoologists to think here was a specimen of goodness knows what with the coat of a mammal the feet of an aquatic bird poison spurs like a reptile and what could only be an egg-laying aperture the zoologists first and quite natural reaction was one of incredulity and their next was one of anger the so-called animal was a hoax some persons in australia with a misplaced sense of humour were taking advantage of the fact that the continent was still so strange and unexplored and had fastened together parts of creatures of different genera to make this preposterous thing

after the zoologists had submitted the creature to the most minute
and scrupulous investigation they had to admit that the creature was
genuine no one had pieced it together as they previously suspected but
how were they to classify it what genus did it belong to was it a reptile
with mammalian characteristics or was it a mammal with reptilian
characteristics or was it part reptile part mammal and part bird

the controversy among scientists raged for decade after decade
different scientific names were suggested but none was satisfactory to
the general public however the creature was the 'duckbill platypus' and
that was that

in 1884 more than eighty years after the first specimen was sent to
britain actual eggs laid by the platypus and another australian species
the spiny ant-eater were found it was not until the twentieth century
that the life of the duckbill platypus was intimately studied we know
that it is an australian aquatic animal which lives in fresh water in
temperatures ranging from that of tropical streams to cold highland
lakes how to classify it however is another matter is it a mammal a
reptile or just a duckbill platypus

John Loughran

Answering comprehension questions on the passage

Work from your own correctly punctuated passage.

1   In what century was Australia discovered?
2   Use the phrases 'to cap it all' and 'goodness knows what' in
     sentences that will clearly illustrate their meaning.
3   What is a zoologist?
4   What kind of bird is an aquatic bird?
5   Put into your own words what the zoologists' first reaction was,
     and why.
6   What is the antonym of 'incredulity'?
7   What was the zoologists' second reaction, and why?
8   Explain with examples the difference between a continent and a
     country.
9   State clearly what you would do if you submitted something to the
     most minute and scrupulous examination.
10   Explain what a misplaced sense of humour is.

11 What did the zoologists find after examining the creature?
12 Why for many decades were the zoologists unable to find a satisfactory scientific name for the creature?
13 (a) What do you understand by the term 'genus'?
    (b) How is the word 'genus' connected with the word 'general'?
14 Mention some of the characteristics which distinguish mammals from reptiles.
15 What is the point of similarity between the duckbill platypus and the spiny ant-eater?
16 What synonyms could be substituted for these in the sentences in which they occur? outlandish, dispatched, dense, secrete, aperture, hoax, submitted, minute, scrupulous, controversy, decade, intimately
17 Use the words themselves in sentences which will clearly illustrate their meaning.

Writing-up notes and making a précis

1 Work from your own punctuated passage, and make brief notes of the story about the platypus.
2 Use your notes to tell the story in your own words. (Do not consult the passage while you are writing.)
3 Make a précis of the passage in 150 words.
4 Look up 'mammal', 'reptile', 'spiny ant-eater', and make brief notes.
5 Use your notes to write a clear and orderly account of what you have found out.

Spellings and vocabulary

1 The words listed at the top of page 109 have been used in Unit 7.
    (a) Test with your neighbour that you can spell the words correctly.
    (b) Learn those you misspelled, and test yourselves again.
    (c) Put the words that may give you difficulty into your notebook for future learning.

I	II	III	IV
behaviour	initiate	neighbours	communicate
amphitheatre	periphery	labyrinth	route
proprietress	cautious	reconnaissance	troglodytes
equipped	territory	specialised	speleologist
encountered	vandalism	casual	classified
secrete	mammalian	incredulity	scrupulous
reptilian	controversy	specimen	intimately

2   Use these words in sentences that will clearly illustrate their meaning: initiate, amphitheatre, periphery, reconnaissance, troglodytes, specialised, secrete, scrupulous, controversy, specimen.

3   Write the adverbial form of these adjectives: cautious, casual, scrupulous.

4   Use the adverbs in sentences that will clearly illustrate their meaning.

5   Write the adjectival form of these nouns: neighbour, periphery, territory, mammal, reptile.

6   Use the adjectives in sentences that will clearly illustrate their meaning.

Essay topics

1   Space Travel.

2   My Favourite Magazines.

3   The Job I Should Like To Do.

4   Write a humorous story about someone carefully following instructions to do something, but nevertheless getting into a real mess.

5   'Women's Lib!' What does it mean to you, and what are your reasons for supporting or opposing it?

6   What criticisms have you of the presentation of news on the radio *or* on television *or* in the newspapers? What changes would you make, and why?

Unit 8

The language of business letters

A business letter should be written in formal language, i.e. language that is impersonal, objective, careful, and correct in the sense that it avoids words and expressions that are used only in speech, and in letters which are not business letters.

A business letter should contain all the details necessary for the business to be carried out, and deal with its business as clearly and briefly as possible.

Writing business letters gives us good practice in using formal language which is clear, brief and to the point.

Discussion on formal and informal language

Discuss the meaning of the words we have used above to describe formal language. Can you think of any other words that could be used to describe it?

On what other occasions, apart from business letters, ought we to use formal language?

What words could be used to describe informal language? When would we use it?

Discuss the various kinds of letters other than business letters people write. Find words to describe the degree of formality or informality that would make each letter appropriate and effective.

Hints on setting out and writing a business letter

1   Put your own legibly written, correctly punctuated and dated address on the right at the top of the letter, as you do in your personal letters.

2   Write the full business address on the left below where your own ends.
3   Begin the letter formally, e.g. Dear Sirs, Dear Mrs Ashton. (If you do use the name of a person in the business, put it and the position held, at the beginning of the address, e.g. Mrs Ashton, The Manageress.)
4   State your business as clearly and briefly as possible, but make sure that you have included all the details which will enable the recipient to act on your letter.
5   End the letter formally, 'Yours truly', unless the letter begins with a name, in which case end 'Yours sincerely'.
6   Sign your full name. This ensures that the person answering your letter is able to address you correctly according to your sex.

Here are two examples of business letters correctly set out and written.

---

13 Lockley Rd
Dunmow
Essex
11 Sept. 1979

Sander and Kay Ltd.
Barlby Road
London W10 GBU

Dear Sirs
    Please send me one pair of dark blue Sleep Easy pyjamas, size 36, for which I enclose a postal order for £___ as requested to cover cost and postage.
                    Yours faithfully,
                    Alan Gardner

Sander & Kay Ltd
Barlby Road
London W10 GBU

21 Sept. 1979

Dear Mr Gardner

Thank you for your order. Please find enclosed one
pair of dark blue Sleep Easy pyjamas, size 36, as
requested.

We trust they will give you complete satisfaction,
and we look forward to receiving your further orders.

Yours faithfully,

Janice Goodall

PP. Sales Manager

Alan Gardner Esq.
13 Lockley Road
Dunmow
Essex

Discussion

Why is it useful to include the full postal address of the business, set out on the left at the top of the letter, as in our first example?

A letter from a firm usually includes on the left at the bottom of the letter the full postal address of the person to whom the letter is addressed. Why?

It is wrong to sign a letter with 'Mr', 'Mrs', 'Miss' or 'Ms' in front of one's name. How, and for what reason, could they be included?

Practice in writing business letters in appropriate language

1   You like the pyjamas you have just received from Sander & Kay Ltd. You find, however, that they have a small hole in the jacket, and you decide to return them. Write an appropriate letter to enclose in the parcel.

2   Draw an envelope, 15 cm by 11 cm. Address it to the firm exactly as recommended by the Post Office.

3   The firm promptly and courteously replaces the pyjamas. Write the letter the Sales Manager sends you.

4   You find the pyjamas so comfortable and such good value that you order another pair, but of a different colour. You also acknowledge how much you appreciated the firm's replying so promptly and courteously. Write the appropriate letter.

5   Write business letters ordering one article each from the firms whose advertisements are reprinted on the following page. (Check them to make sure that they are satisfactory, i.e. formal, clear and as brief as possible without omitting any essential detail.)

Examples of unsatisfactory business letters

25 Marlborough Rd
Salisbury
SA3 4UR
18·10·79

Dear Sir,

My aunt, who is now very old well over eighty in fact, has been suddenly taken ill and I have to go at once and look after her she has no one else. Last week I wrote you and ordered a new coat this I now cannot afford as I have to spend the money on the journey to my aunt as well as looking after her.

Yours in haste,
Miss Alice Fay

The Gables
12 East St
Totnes
Devon
6th Feb. 1980

Blatchford & Co., Ltd

Dear Mr Freeman,

My mother-in-law, who was staying with us for only a few days (fortunately you know what mothers-in-law are!) should have gone back yesterday but has now suddenly decided to stay a few more days heaven knows why. As if this wasn't enough my wife has to go off early next week to look after her sister, who has gone down with chick-pox of all things I'm very sorry therefore that I can't meet you to discuss the business deal tomorrow as we arranged we should do when I spoke to you on the telephone two days ago.

Yours truly,
A S Bailey

Green Hedges
Blandford
Dorset
15th August 1979

Garden Sheds Ltd

Dear Sir,

I saw your advertisement for garden sheds quite by chance last week when I was spending an idle moment leafing through 'How Does Your Garden Grow?', which incidentally I think is the best of all gardening magazines. I have an unsightly corner, measuring nine feet by five, and when I saw your advertisement it suddenly occurred to me that I could kill two birds with one stone as the saying goes.

Do you possess a shed which would do for this site? If so I should be glad if you would please send me full particulars. If not any advice you may be able to offer will be gratefully received.

Very sincerely yours,
Ada Flower (Miss)

Lockley, Ltd
Union Street
Exeter

5.5.80

Dear Madam,

We beg to acknowledge receipt of your communication of 29th ult. in which you state that the goods consigned to you by us were received in a damaged condition.

We are totally unable to understand why this should be so as the goods complained of were thoroughly checked before they left our store and found to be in perfect condition. In addition they were adequately packed by our very experienced and skilled packing department.

In view of the above we cannot accept any liability whatsoever and respectfully suggest that you communicate without further delay with British Rail and lodge your complaint with them.

Yours faithfully,
J. Norse
(Sales Manager)

Mrs V. Styles
The Haven
6 The Crescent
Cardiff CF1 4ED

Discussion

Ignore the fact that the four letters are business letters, and concentrate on their clarity and correctness.

What improvements to the punctuation would you make to remove ambiguities and make the sense clearer?

What mistakes in grammar have been made, and how should they be put right?

How would you describe the language in which the letters are written? Compare it with the language in which a business letter should be written.

How should a business letter deal with its business? How do these letters deal with theirs?

What cuts and alterations would you make to turn them into satisfactory business letters? Pay attention to the internal addresses, and the beginnings and endings, as well as the language and contents.

Written work

1 In what kind of language should a business letter be written?
2 How should a business letter deal with its business, and why?
3 Make satisfactory versions of each of the four business letters we have discussed (pp. 115–16).
4 Turn each of the letters on the next three pages into a satisfactory business letter.

(a)

Bulb Farm Ltd,
Boston,
Lincs.

12th Sept.1979

Dear Sir,

   Further to your esteemed order.   We have great pleasure in
forwarding under separate cover the following bulbs.

                    1 doz. Darwin tulips
                    3 doz. mixed Crocus
                    2 doz. Boston Pride daffs

       Trusting to give every satisfaction.

                         We remain,
                         Yours faithfully,

                         G. Briggs.
                         (for Bulb Farm Ltd)

(b)

                              The Orchard
                              Skelton Court
                              Ruislip
                                Middx.
                              4th March 1980

Dear Sir,
       I notice from your advertisement in my Sunday
paper that your sale is commencing in a fortnights
time. As we have been married over ten years now
I am in urgent need of some new bed linen and
towels, and one or two other items, and I should be
extremely obliged if you would very kindly
send me your Sales Brochure as advertised.

              Yours sincerely,

              J. Townsend.

118

(c)

J V Harris & Co. Ltd.,
High Street
Crediton
Devon
6th June 1980

Ideal Tractors Ltd.,
Marsh Barton Estate,
Exeter EX2 12PA

Dear Sirs,

We have received an enquiry from a customer, a very good farmer who farms some 350 acres locally. He needs a good general-purpose heavy tractor, able to perform efficiently all that is normally required of such a machine, and a small, handy, easily operated tractor for use on a small area of the land not suitable to be worked by the heavier and more clumsy machine.

Please be kind enough to let us have your suggestions as to what would suit him best, and send us full specifications, prices, and the terms on which you would be able to supply the machines.

Our customer, who is well known for his speed and efficiency, is anxious to come to a decision as soon as possible, and we shall accordingly be glad to receive a prompt reply.

Yours faithfully
A N Harris
(Manager)

(d)

Cosy Nook
Friars Road
Chard
Somerset
12.12.79

Dear Mr Sweet,

You may remember that Mr and Mrs Willis stayed at your boarding house last year, in August, I think it was. Well, they are our closest friends and when they came back from their holiday they told us they had a really marvellous time. They praised you up to the skies and swore they had never stayed in a better place.

This decided us and we agreed that we must stay with you next year if possible. We are five in a family, my husband and I, and our three children. We should require only two bedrooms, as the children are all quite small. The two boys could sleep in a double bed, and Baby, who is only eighteen months old, could sleep in a cot if necessary.

Our holidays are from the 10th - 24th August, and we do hope you will be able to have us. Please let us know your terms for full board when you write.

Yours in anticipation,

J. Simmonds (Mrs)

(e)

10 The Street
Rayne
Braintree
Essex
4.1.80

Messrs Green & Green,

Dear Sirs,

My neighbour grows the loveliest flowers and vegetables every year, always far better than mine. This year I at last got round to asking him why and he said it was because he only used the best seeds. When I asked him whose these were, he gave me your name and address. This is why I am now writing to ask you to send me your new seed and flower catalogue, as this year I intend starting off on the right foot. I only hope my results will be as good as his.

Yours sincerely,
Judith Jones (Miss)

5   Draw envelopes, 15 cm by 11 cm, and address them exactly as the Post Office advocates to:
   i. Ideal Tractors—letter (c), page 119;
   ii. Mrs Sweet—letter (d), page 119;
   iii. The Sales Manager, Lockley Ltd—second letter, page 116.

Making sure : using a pair of commas, dashes or brackets to enclose words in parenthesis

Words in parenthesis are words which have been inserted in a sentence to add extra information. The sentence is grammatically complete without them, so they can be taken out of the sentence without impairing its sense.

The punctuation marks used to enclose words in parenthesis are a pair of commas, a pair of dashes and a pair of brackets.

(a) A pair of commas

The most usual punctuation mark used to enclose words in parenthesis is a pair of commas. When you write such sentences as these, beware of omitting the second comma.

Terry, unfortunately, cannot be with us.

The birds, all parakeets, were huddled together in one corner of the aviary.

Vina, her basket crammed with groceries, was walking very slowly homewards.

The car, a battered old Morris Minor, had eight people in it.

The rabbit, which was lying huddled on the grass, tried in vain to get up and walk away as I approached it.

This apple, which I found on the ground, was much sweeter than those you gave me.

(b) A pair of dashes

Words in parenthesis can be enclosed in a pair of dashes when the writer wishes to draw attention to the words—to make their insertion in the sentence appear sudden and dramatic.

A pair of dashes is also used to enclose words in parenthesis which are themselves separated by commas.

The car—a battered old Morris Minor—had eight people in it.

Jill—her face purple with rage—sprang forward.

Garry—what a clown he is!—began to tell us about another of his mad doings.

The waves were mountainous—never in all my years at sea had I seen bigger—and I feared they would overwhelm the ship.

The lamb—bleating pitifully, and already beginning to bleed—was hanging from the eagle's talons as the huge bird rose above the trees.

They could see the horses—neighing, stamping, rearing, dashing to and fro—but the men who had corralled them had vanished.

(c) A pair of brackets

A pair of brackets encloses words in parenthesis which do not really belong to the main sentence (added as if by an afterthought), or which are a direct explanation of the words that precede the brackets.

The effect of the brackets is to hide the words from the reader's attention, sometimes making them into a kind of confidential aside.

When the parenthetic words are a complete sentence, the punctuation mark that ends the sentence is placed inside the brackets.

Study the sentences in the last paragraph (p. 43).

The model is easy to assemble (see enclosed instructions).

Antimacassars (coverings for the backs of chairs) were very fashionable in Victorian times.

Be most careful what you say when you talk to him. (Under no circumstances must you mention me!)

Written work

1   Use a pair of commas to insert words in parenthesis into these sentences.
  (a) Joe ate steadily.
  (b) The women were standing in a circle.
  (c) Fosya and Amargit were hurrying along the pavement.
  (d) Their mother always had their dinner ready on time.
2   Copy these sentences, correcting the punctuation where necessary.
  (a) Roger fortunately for him, found his purse.
  (b) Just as he approached me, however he slipped and fell.
  (c) The twins, as you would expect were first in the queue.
  (d) We felt very relieved that our neighbour, now very old and infirm was going to live with her daughter.
3   Use a pair of dashes to insert parenthetic words in these sentences, thus making their insertion appear abrupt and dramatic.

(a) The tiger charged.

(b) The snakes were trying to get out of the pit.

(c) Wendy was still standing where I had left her.

(d) Annie ate steadily.

(e) The twins were first in the queue.

4 Copy these sentences, inserting a pair of dashes to draw attention to the words in parenthesis.

(a) Dale screamed the pain was more than he could bear and went on screaming.

(b) The two men where had they been hiding jumped on our bicycles and rode away.

(c) Everything of value in the room, clock, ornaments, pictures, even the carpet and chairs had been taken.

(d) The twins nobody who knows them will be at all surprised were first in the queue.

5 Use a pair of brackets to add to these sentences words which do not really belong to them, or which are a direct explanation of the words that precede the brackets.

(a) Study the paragraph, then answer these questions

(b) First consult the map

(c) Take great care when you are assembling the model

(d) A good deal of modern poetry is written in free verse

(e) His dialect makes him difficult to understand

(f) Duckbill platypuses are rare

6 Copy these sentences, correcting the punctuation where necessary.

(a) Turn to the poem (p. 26)

(b) You should have no difficulty finding the house (See the sketch map enclosed).

(c) It was quite obvious he thought he knew me, but I was convinced I had never seen him before. (I never did find out who he was).

(d) First identify the long and short syllables (What are long and short syllables)?

(e) The kit has been dispatched in perfect condition. (Please check that all the parts are present and intact before you begin to assemble the aircraft).

Essay topics

1 Describe some of your visits to the dentist.
2 Boats.
3 People today often speak of the 'generation gap'. By this they mean that older people and teenagers do not understand one another, and that this leads to all kinds of problems, difficulties and misunderstandings. Discuss examples from your own experience, and suggest, if you can, how the 'gap' might be overcome.
4 My Favourite Season of the Year.
5 Describe and discuss heroes and heroines you admire.
6 Phone-ins.

Unit 9

Describing and restricting adjective clauses

Adjective clauses which are inserted into a sentence to add extra information about a noun or pronoun are enclosed in a pair of commas, dashes or brackets. The sentence is grammatically complete without such parenthetic clauses, and so they can be removed without altering its sense.

Adjective clauses which restrict the meaning of the noun or pronoun are not enclosed between a pair of punctuation marks, because they are an essential part of the meaning of the sentence.

The rabbit, which was lying huddled on the grass, tried in vain to get up and walk away.
The rabbit which was lying huddled on the grass tried in vain to get up and walk away.

The old man, who was bent almost double, was glad to sit down.
The old man who was bent almost double was glad to sit down.

The children, who are all from the same school, come here at Easter.
The children who are all from the same school come here at Easter.

In the first of each pair of sentences, the parenthetic clause may be left out without altering the meaning of the sentence.

The second sentence of each pair implies that there was more than one rabbit, one old man or one group of children, and that it is a particular rabbit, old man or group that is being referred to. The meaning is restricted to that particular rabbit, old man or group. The clause could not therefore be removed without altering the meaning of the whole sentence.

Similarly, a descriptive adjective clause coming at the end of a sentence is separated by a comma, while a restrictive clause is not.

We dislike buses, which are noisy.
We dislike buses which are noisy.

Take it to the office, which deals with such things.
Take it to the office which deals with such things.

Discussion

Put into your own words the difference in meaning between the sentences in each pair.

Restrictive clauses are also known as defining clauses. Why is this?

Written work

1 Add correctly punctuated descriptive adjective clauses to each of these sentences.
    (a) The boy trod on some glass and cut his foot.
    (b) The python slowly uncurled itself from the branch.
    (c) The babies are all looking very content.
    (d) The traffic had by now completely jammed the street.
    (e) We have been treated very well.
2 Rewrite the sentences so that the clauses become restrictive, not describing.
3 Explain the difference in meaning between the sentences in Nos 1 and 2.
4 Explain the difference in meaning between these pairs of sentences.
    (a) I hate trains which are dirty.
         I hate trains, which are dirty.
    (b) Take it back to the butcher who sold it to you.
         Take it back to the butcher, who sold it to you.
    (c) Give it to the beggar who has only one leg.
         Give it to the beggar, who has only one leg.

Personification

Personification is a figure of speech in which something is personified, i.e. treated as if it were a person.

We use personification naturally and without thinking, as we do other kinds of metaphorical language.

The yacht bounded forward, her every sail straining

The grass was hammered flat by the gale.

The car screamed to a stop.

Personification is used in poetry to increase the impact words have on us. Sometimes whatever is personified is written with a capital letter, sometimes not.

Examples

How many thousand of my poorest subjects
Are at this hour asleep. O sleep! O gentle sleep!
Nature's soft nurse, how have I frighted thee,
That thou no more wilt weigh my eyelids down
And steep my senses in forgetfulness?
From *Henry IV, Part Two*, by William Shakespeare

The glories of our blood and state
Are shadows, not substantial things;
There is no armour against Fate;
Death lays his icy hand on Kings:
Sceptre and Crown
Must tumble down,
And in the dust be equal made
With the poor crooked scythe and spade.
From 'Death the Leveller', by James Shirley

Sport that wrinkled Care derides,
And Laughter holding both his sides.
From 'L'Allegro', by John Milton

O wild west wind, thou breath of Autumn's being,
Thou, from whose unseen presence the leaves dead
Are driven, like ghosts from an enchantress fleeing.
From 'Ode to the West Wind', by Percy Bysshe Shelley

And the startled little waves that leap
In fiery ringlets from their sleep.
From 'Meeting at Night', by Robert Browning

THE BEACH

The beach is a quarter of golden fruit,
a soft ripe melon
sliced to a half-moon curve,
having a thick green rind
of jungle growth;
and the sea devours it
with its sharp,
sharp white teeth.
By W. Hart-Smith

Discussion

Discuss the personifications, and what they contribute to the poetry.

We have dealt with two other figures of speech, metaphor and simile. Which is being used in the first five lines of W. Hart-Smith's poem? How would you change this figure of speech into another one? If this were done, what would the poem gain or lose?

What is being personified in the last three lines of the same poem?

Discuss in detail how the two figures of speech used in the poem are combined to create a vivid and original image of the scene.

What kind of verse is the poem written in, and what makes it so?

Compare this prose description with the poem, and say with your reasons which you prefer.

The cove was shaped like a half-moon. The sand was soft and golden, the colour of a ripe melon. Behind it lay the dense green jungle. The tide was coming in, and its white edge was gradually covering the beach.

What do you notice about the rhyme scheme of James Shirley's stanza (p. 128)? What does it, combined with the metre, contribute to the effect the lines have?

Why do you think the verse in which Shakespeare wrote his plays is called blank verse?

Written work

1 Write sentences in which you personify each of these: icy-cold rain, famine, time, a forest, a racing car, intense heat, a river, winter, fear.
2 What does Shakespeare personify sleep as?
3 In what sense is sleep what Shakespeare says it is?
4 What are personified in the third and fourth lines of Shirley's poem?
5 Use these personifications in dramatic sentences of your own.
6 What are personified in the last four lines of Shirley's poem, and what do they stand for?

7   What are personified in Milton's couplet?

8   Use the personifications in interesting sentences of your own.

9   What does Shelley say the wind is? Add your own opinion of this personification.

10   Study the way Browning personifies the waves in his couplet. Taking this as your model, write a paragraph in which you personify waves, sand, breeze and the moon.

11   Copy the stanza from 'Death the Leveller'. Mark the rhyme scheme and metre. Comment on the interplay of metre, speech rhythms and rhyme scheme.

12   Discuss W. Hart-Smith's 'The Beach', and the effect it had on you. (Begin by saying what kind of a poem it is, and how many lines in how many stanzas it contains.)

Onomatopoeia

Many words were originally formed to imitate or suggest by their sound what they stood for, e.g. phew, miaow, hiss, bang, clatter, plop, swish, sizzle, cuckoo.

Onomatopoeia is the name given to the deliberate use of such words. The adjectives used to describe such words is 'onomatopoeic'.

Discussion

Discuss the above examples, and others of your own. Try dividing them into two classes: those obviously originally made up to imitate sounds or movements; those you think might have been made up to suggest the thing itself.

As we know, writers of comic verse, e.g. Lewis Carroll, often make up onomatopoeic words of their own. What examples can you remember from him and other verse writers?

Have some fun making up some onomatopoeic nonsense words of your own.

Poets often use onomatopoeia to echo and suggest and thereby enrich the meaning of what they write. Sometimes they combine it with alliteration and rhyme, sometimes not. Here are some examples to read aloud and discuss.

Examples

Five miles meandering with a mazy motion
Through wood and dale the sacred river ran,
Then reached the caverns measureless to man,
And sank in tumult to a lifeless ocean.
    From 'Kubla Khan', by Samuel Taylor Colcridge

SIR BEDIVERE CARRIES THE WOUNDED KING ARTHUR TO THE
LAKE

Dry clashed his harness in the icy caves
And barren chasms, and all to left and right
The bare black cliffs clanged round him, as he based
His feet on juts of slippery crag that rang
Sharp-smitten with the dint of armed heels—
And on a sudden, lo! the level lake,
And the long glories of the winter moon.
    From 'Morte d'Arthur', by Alfred, Lord Tennyson

Myriads of rivulets hurrying through the lawn,
The moan of doves in immemorial elms,
And murmuring of innumerable bees.
    From 'The Princess', by Alfred, Lord Tennyson

Forget six counties overhung with smoke,
Forget the snorting steam and piston stroke,
Forget the spreading of the hideous town;
Think rather of the pack-horse on the down,
And dream of London, small and white and clean,
The clear Thames bordered by its garden green.
    From 'The Wanderers', by William Morris

After the first powerful plain manifesto,
The black statement of pistons, without more fuss
But gliding like a queen, she leaves the station.
    From 'The Express', by Stephen Spender

1   Use these onomatopoeic words in amusing sentences:
    scrumptious, cruddled, screech, burbled, waffle, groan, scritch,
    doodling, galumphing, clack.
2   Use these onomatopoeic words in interesting sentences:
    scintillate, meandering, susurration, clashed, clanged, lazily,
    gloom, gleam, dwindled, whines.
3   Use some of the onomatopoeic words made up in *Discussion*, page
    130, in amusing sentences.
4   Try making up some comic verses, using existing and made-up
    onomatopoeic words.
5   Discuss what the onomatopoeia, alliteration and rhyme
    contribute to the effect each quotation on pages 131–2 has.
6   Shakespeare wrote many of his plays in the reign of Queen
    Elizabeth I of England.
    (a) Look up Shakespeare and Queen Elizabeth I, and make notes
    of some of the important facts you find interesting.
    (b) Turn your notes into clear and informative prose accounts.
7   Look at the photograph on page 127, then discuss a Shakespeare
    play you have seen.
8   (a) Look up and make notes on any aspects of Elizabethan life
    that interest you, e.g. dress, sports and pastimes, ships, voyages of
    discovery, battles, weapons.
    (b) Use your notes to write interesting prose accounts of your
    findings.
9   Reread Tennyson's lines from 'Morte d'Arthur', then:
    (a) look up and make notes on the Knights of the Round Table.
    (b) turn your notes into informative prose accounts.
10 Look at the photograph of the steam engine, then write in any way
    you please about steam railway engines, or about railways.

Criticising a poem

As we know, a criticism of a literary work consists of an assessment of
both its good and bad points, of its strengths as well as its weaknesses.

Our criticism of a poem should therefore consist of two parts.
i. We should first give an appreciation of the poem. This consists of stating with our reasons what, in our opinion, are its successful and pleasing features.
ii. Secondly, we should deal in the same way with its less successful and less pleasing features.

Poets, by their choice of words, try to share their experiences, thoughts and feelings with us. Our criticism should make a reasoned personal assessment of how well they have succeeded. Remember that any such personal assessment is all the more persuasive when we back up the appreciative and adverse points we make with quotations from the text.

Images and imagery

Poets often use words to create images, because it is through images that they can best convey what they experience, think and feel. Their imagery may be expressed in metaphorical or literal language, or embodied in such figures of speech as metaphor, simile or personification.

Poetry is made with words. To heighten the effect the poem has on the reader, poets choose their words most skilfully. paying attention to their sound and movement, as well as to their meaning, shades of meaning and the associations they carry with them.

They also use words in rhythms that are subtly different from those of prose. They may use metre with or without rhyme, rhyme without metre, or free verse, all enriched by alliteration and onomatopoeia.

Commenting on poets' images—their imagery—is a most important part of the criticism of a poem. Here are some examples of imagery, including a complete poem composed of images.

Examples

This royal throne of kings, this scepter'd isle,
This earth of majesty, this seat of Mars.
From *Richard II,* Act II, Scene 1, by William Shakespeare

And like a bunch of ragged carrots stand
The short swoll'n fingers of thy gouty hand.
    John Donne

Sometimes whoever seeks abroad may find
Thee sitting careless on a granary floor,
Thy hair soft-lifted by the winnowing wind.
    From 'Ode to Autumn', by John Keats

The Assyrian came down like the wolf on the fold,
And his cohorts were gleaming in purple and gold;
And the sheen of their spears was like stars on the sea,
When the blue wave rolls nightly on deep Galilee.
    From 'The Destruction of Sennacherib', by George Gordon
    Byron, Lord Byron

The rain set early in tonight,
The sullen wind was soon awake,
It tore the elm-tops down for spite,
And did its worst to vex the lake.
    From 'Porphyria's Lover', by Robert Browning

And swordlike was the sound of the iron wind,
And as a breaking battle was the sea.
    From 'Tristan and Iseult', by Algernon Charles Swinburne

The wind was a torrent of darkness among the gusty trees,
The moon was a ghostly galleon tossed upon cloudy seas,
The road was a ribbon of moonlight over the purple moor.
    From 'The Highwayman', by Alfred Noyes

The grass is happy
To run like a sea, to be glossed like a mink's fur
By polishing wind.
    From 'Hay', by Ted Hughes

Timothy Winters comes to school
With eyes as wide as a football pool,
Ears like bombs and teeth like splinters:
A blitz of a boy is Timothy Winters.
From 'Timothy Winters', by Charles Causley

THE RIVER IN MARCH

Now the river is rich, but her voice is low.
It is her Mighty Majesty the sea
Travelling among the villages incognito.

Now the river is poor. No song, just a thin mad whisper.
The winter floods have ruined her.
She squats between draggled banks, fingering her rags and rubbish.

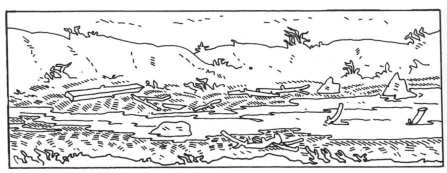

And now the river is rich. A deep choir.
It is the lofty clouds, that work in heaven,
Going on their holiday to the sea.

The river is poor again. All her bones are showing.
Through a dry wig of bleached flotsam she peers up ashamed
From her slum of sticks.

Now the river is rich, collecting shawls and minerals.
Rain brought fatness, but she takes ninety-nine per cent
Leaving the fields just one per cent to survive on.

And now she is poor. Now she is East wind sick.
She huddles in holes and corners. The brassy sun gives her a headache.
She has lost all her fish. And she shivers.

But now once more she is rich. She is viewing her lands.
A hoard of king-cups spills from her folds, it blazes, it cannot be hidden.
A salmon, a sow of solid silver,

Bulges to glimpse it.

Ted Hughes

Discussion on imagery

Discuss the images in the above examples. Which are embodied in
metaphorical language, and which in literal language? Which images
are metaphors, which similes and which personifications?

Discuss also the use of alliteration and onomatopoeia, and what they
contribute to the imagery.

In Ted Hughes's poem, how effective are the images in conveying
aspects of the river and its life? Which of his images gave you most
pleasure, and why?

Written work

1   Comment in detail on the verse form, language and imagery of the
    quotations on pages 134–6, excluding Ted Hughes's long poem.
2   What part of the river is Ted Hughes referring to in the first stanza
    of 'The River in March', and in what kind of weather?
3   Use 'incognito' in a sentence to illustrate clearly its meaning.
4   Describe what you would see, and why, if you were looking at the
    river as imaged in the second stanza.
5   What does Ted Hughes imply that the clouds are actually doing?
6   What made the river poor again, then rich again (stanza 5), and
    how do we know?
7   What could be done to prevent the river taking 'ninety-nine per
    cent' of the rain?

8   Explain the circumstances that made the river sick.
9   What must have happened to enable the river to 'view her lands'?
10 How do you explain the presence of the salmon when the river had 'lost all her fish'?
11 Of what kind of verse is the poem an example, and what makes it so?
12 Apply all the knowledge you have gained to write a detailed criticism of the poem.

MY MOTHER SAW A DANCING BEAR

My mother saw a dancing bear
By the schoolyard, a day in June.
The keeper stood with chain and bar
And whistle-pipe, and played a tune.

And bruin lifted up its head
And lifted up its dusty feet,
And all the children laughed to see
It caper in the summer heat.

They watched as for the Queen it died.
They watched it march. They watched it halt.
They heard the keeper as he cried,
'Now, roly-poly!' 'Somersault!'

And then, my mother said, there came
The keeper with a begging-cup,
The bear with burning coat of fur,
Shaming the laughter to a stop.

They paid a penny for the dance,
But what they saw was not the show;
Only, in bruin's aching eyes,
Far-distant forests, and the snow.

Charles Causley

13 Write a similarly detailed criticism of Charles Causley's poem.
14 Point out and comment on some of the chief differences in
    technique and language between 'The River in March' and 'My
    Mother Saw a Dancing Bear'.
15 Compare and contrast the technique and language of the haiku
    and senryū (pages 47–8), and Edwin Morgan's two poems
    (pp. 86–7) with that of the two poems you discussed in No. 14.

Making sure I: using the apostrophe

i. *Apostrophe* s *('*s*) is used to form the possessive singular of all nouns, and the
possessive plural of nouns not ending in* s.

He was given Bharat's cricket bat.

The dog's barking alerted us to the danger.

The children's outing has been postponed.

ii. s *apostrophe* (s'*) is used to form the possessive plural of nouns ending in* s.

The girls' races were most entertaining.

We noticed that the babies' rattles were all made of plastic.

iii. *Apostrophe* s *('*s*) is used to form the possessive singular of compound words
and titles, and of a group of names.*

His father-in-law's garden was a delight to see.

The Mayor of Adelaide's car was huge.

What used to be the Emperor of China's throne is in this museum.

iv. *The apostrophe shows where letters or numbers have been missed out in the
contractions used in writing conversation, and in informal writing* (see page 33).

'I'll send it soon, but you'll have to wait a few days as I'm very busy at present,'
Prakesh said.

'They weren't told,' said Rosemary, frowning, 'so they couldn't do what you've just said they ought to have done.'

The Second World War began in '39.

I'm sorry I haven't written before, but I've been very busy swotting for exams. I should've done, and I hope you'll forgive me . . .

I admire David Broome and Harvey Smith's horsemanship.

NB The ordinary plurals of nouns are written without an apostrophe.

The dogs are barking loudly.

The girls are working hard.

There were at least fifty babies there.

Making sure II: possessive pronouns

The six possessive pronouns, *his, hers, ours, yours, theirs* and *mine* show possession by their form alone.

The black pen is his, and the red pen is hers.

Ours is over there, but we can't see yours anywhere.

Those bicycles are theirs, but I haven't brought mine.

Written work

1   Write the possessive of five singular nouns.
2   Use the five possessives in interesting sentences.
3   How is the possessive of all plural nouns not ending in *s* formed?
4   Write the possessives of three plural nouns not ending in *s*.
5   Use the three possessives in interesting sentences.
6   How is the possessive of plural nouns ending in *s* formed?

7   Write the possessive of five plural nouns ending in *s*.

8   Use the five possessives in interesting sentences.

9   People sometimes confuse the possessive of a noun with its plural by writing the plural with an apostrophe. What test could they carry out to distinguish the one from the other?

10 Show that any three of the possessives you have used in sentences are in fact possessives by applying the test.

11 Copy and correct these sentences.

  (a) Belindas pen is broken.

  (b) The childrens's shoes were missing.

  (c) St Peters Square was filled with people.

  (d) The babies cries filled the room.

  (e) The butterflies' were too numerous to count.

  (f) We have a months holiday this year.

  (g) The womans laughter was infectious.

  (h) Our cats favourite food is fish.

Essay topics

1   Rights and Responsibilities.

2   Popularity.

3   Being Old in Great Britain Today.

4   Discuss what you hope to be doing in five years from now.

5   'The present age is the best age to be living in.' Discuss this statement.

6   Describe to someone who has never visited us before what it is like living in the town *or* in the country.

Unit 10

Common errors and confusions

1   *The Infinitive.*

The infinitive is identifiable by the 'to' in front of it: to travel (pres. inf.); to be travelling (continuous pres. inf.); to have travelled (past inf.); to have been travelling (continuous past inf.).

In our writing we should avoid putting an adverb between the 'to' and the infinitive it identifies, e.g. *to go boldly*, or *boldly to go*, not *to boldly go*.

This advice is sometimes expressed as a rule—do not split the infinitive. The so-called rule is a convenient way of putting the advice, provided we remember that there is really no infinitive to split: 'to' points to the infinitive, but is not a part of it.

2   *Take care not to confuse 'can' and 'may'.*

I can come with you. (= am able to)
I may come with you. (= have permission to)

I can eat another bun. (= have room for)
May I have another bun? (= will you allow me)

3   *Negatives.*

i. *Use only one negative in a sentence.*

Bill could not have any.
or Bill could have none.

He does not possess anything.
or He possesses nothing.

She did not give me any money.
or She gave me no money.

ii. *After a negative, use 'or' to express a negative meaning.*

They do not sing or play.

Julie cannot read or write.

iii. *After a positive, use 'neither . . . nor' to express a negative meaning.*

They neither sing nor play.

Julie can neither read nor write.

4   *Take care not to confuse 'affect' and 'effect'.*

i. *affect (verb) = pretend to have or to be, produce an effect on*

She affected ignorance.

His lungs were affected by the dense smoke.

ii. *effect (noun) = a change resulting from an action or cause, an impression produced on someone*

Smoking has a bad effect on health.

He acts like that only for the effect.

effect (verb) = to bring about, to accomplish

The government effected many changes.

Dr Morgan effected a miraculous cure.

5   *Take care not to use 'annoy' for 'aggravate', which means to make worse.*

Her illness was aggravated by lack of good food.

His offence was aggravated by his rudeness.

6   *'All right' must be written as two words.*

Please don't worry, I shall be quite all right.

'All right, I will go now,' I said quietly.

7   *Do not confuse 'complement' and 'compliment'.*

i. complement = whatever makes something complete

The train has a full complement of passengers.

My new hat complements my outfit.

The second book is complementary to the first.

ii. *compliment = praise*

Her teacher complimented her on her work.

His boss paid him a most unexpected compliment.

They were all most complimentary about my appearance.

8   *'Could have', not 'could of'.*

He could have done it.

They could not have been here yesterday.

9 *Do not confuse 'infer' and 'imply'.*

i. *infer = to reach a conclusion from facts or reasoning*

Am I right to infer that you did not actually go?

We inferred it was a mammal, and our inference was correct.

ii. *imply = to hint; to suggest implicitly*

Tell me in a straightforward way what you are implying.

The beauty of the painting implies a skilled artist.

10 *Do not confuse to 'lie' (down) and to 'lay'.*

i. *to lie (down)*

Lie down and go to sleep.

He lies in the long grass, the sun on his face.

They are so tired that they are going to lie down.

The baby lay on the floor and gurgled. (= past tense of 'lie')

They have lain all day in the sun.

ii. *to lay = to deposit*

Father always lays his bets before lunch.

That hen lays regularly every day.

They have laid the carpet very well.

11 *phenomenon (sing.) = a fact, occurrence or change perceived by the senses or the mind. The plural is 'phenomena'.*

In Scandinavia, snow is a very common phenomenon in winter.

The phenomena kept on occurring, yet no one could account for them.

12 *Do not confuse 'prevaricate' and 'procrastinate'.*

i. *prevaricate = to lie, to speak evasively*

You are prevaricating—I know you were not present.

He is prevaricating about what he did yesterday.

ii. *procrastinate = to postpone action, to be dilatory*

She has procrastinated for a whole week now.

We shall lose the opportunity if we procrastinate any further.

Written work

1　Use these adverbs with suitable infinitives in interesting sentences: boldly, quietly, slyly, conscientiously, soothingly.
2　Copy and correct these sentences.
　(a)　Can I have another cup of coffee, please?
　(b)　Can we go now?
　(c)　They have asked permission, and they may stay till ten o'clock.
　(d)　We haven't got none.
　(e)　He hasn't given me no sweets.
　(f)　We neither smoke or drink.
　(g)　They do not know whether to go nor stay.

3　Write sentences which will clearly demonstrate the correct meaning of these words: affect, effect, annoy, aggravate, all right, complement, compliment, could have, infer, imply, prevaricate, procrastinate.

4　Write sentences in which you correctly use the present, future and past tenses of 'lie' (down) and 'lay'.

5　Write sentences in which you use 'phenomenon' and 'phenomena' correctly.

Test yourself

1　Teach not thy parents' mother to extract
The embryo juices of the bird by suction.
The good old lady can that feat enact
Quite irrespective of thy kind instruction.

(a) Summarise the verse in a single sentence.
(b) Copy it, and indicate the metre and rhyme scheme.
(c) How many feet are there in each line?

2　Use these words in sentences which will clearly illustrate their meaning: extract, embryo, feat, enact, irrespective.

3　There was a young girl, a sweet lamb,
Who smiled as she entered a tram.
After she had embarked,
The conductor remarked,
'Your fare'. And she said, 'Yes, I am'.
Anon.

(a) Copy the limerick, and indicate the rhyme scheme and metre.
(b) Explain the pun.
(c) Use the limerick, or another of your own choice, to point out all the rules a limerick must obey to be a limerick.

147

4

> Lucy and Sam would love to see you at their birthday party on November 26th starting at 6 p.m. Good food is promised, followed by a disco, all at 28 Hetherington Avenue. Do come!
>
> Lucy   Sam

Unfortunately, you cannot accept the twins' invitation, though you would like to very much, especially as last year it was such a good party. Write an appropriate reply.

5   Both a very close friend and yourself were invited to Lucy and Sam's birthday party. You were able to go, but your friend had measles and was unable to. You are still not allowed to visit your friend, so you decide to write a cheerful, humorous letter describing the party, which this year was an utter disaster!

6   Draw three envelopes and address them as the Post Office recommends to:
(a) a friend;
(b) a relative or neighbour;
(c) your headteacher.

7   Choose two advertisements from a teenage magazine, or from a newspaper. Write business letters:
(a) ordering the first article;
(b) returning the second because of a defect.

8   Draw and correctly address the envelopes.

9   'My first attempt to skate was a disaster . . .' Write a humorous story with this beginning. Substitute another sport or pastime if you wish.

10　Pause, motorist, pause,
　　Sue Smith lies here.
　　She lit her fag,
　　But forgot to steer.
　　　　　　Anon.

(a) Copy the verse. Put in the rhyme scheme, and comment on the alliteration.

(b) Imagine that you witnessed the accident referred to above, which happened in a spot you know well. Write a clear and factual report of what happened from the time you saw the car to the arrival of the police and ambulance.

11　You are a newspaper reporter. Write the reports suggested by any two of these headlines.
　　(a) TIGER RECAPTURED
　　(b) DANGEROUS CONVICT STILL AT LARGE
　　(c) BOYS TORTURE TRAPPED BIRDS
　　(d) HOUSEWIFE DEFENDS HUNTED STAG

12　Choose two of the following, and write clear and concise instructions which will enable a person who has not done the job previously to carry it out successfully. Assume, however, that the person is familiar with the items or ingredients. Take about three-quarters of a page for your answer:
　　(a) preparing, cooking and serving a hot snack;
　　(b) preparing, dressing and serving a vegetable salad that contains at least five ingredients;
　　(c) checking the battery, oil and water in a car, assuming each item needs attention, and giving instructions for the necessary action;
　　(d) choosing and packing the clothing and articles needed for a stay of five days away from home *either* in town *or* country;
　　(e) washing, rinsing and drying a load of washing at a launderette.

13　Write an objective factual description of two of these:
　　(a) a discotheque;

(b) the premises of a youth club;
(c) a church hall;
(d) the waiting room of a doctor or dentist's surgery;
(e) an open-air swimming pool.

14 Write a personal and subjective description of:
(a) a visit to a doctor or dentist;
(b) a visit to an open-air pool on a chilly, sunless August afternoon.

15 Imagine that you are any two of the persons listed below. Give an account of your feelings as you look back on your previous experience, and forward to what lies ahead:
(a) a farmer or shepherd seeing the last of the winter's snows disappearing;
(b) a pupil on his/her last day of school;
(c) someone who is very keen on winter sports as the season opens;
(d) an emigrant (or immigrant) waiting to embark.

16 Write the conversation that takes place between:
(a) a girl and boy and two visitors from outer space;
(b) a family sitting around the fire, the father reading his son's report—obviously a bad one—his daughter holding hers and looking very pleased.

17 Turn both conversations into reported speech.

18 Copy this passage, putting in the necessary capital letters and punctuation marks.
it seems that human beings since they became human that is have always had an insatiable desire to know this has taken many forms exploration being one we have explored the surface of the earth and we had begun to explore outer space what then remained what was the last great frontier to be explored
two men jacques piccard and donald walsh set out on january 23 1960 to explore that last great frontier to do so they embarked on

Jacques Piccard (on the right) is shown here on board the Trieste. *The other man is his father.*

one of the most perilous journeys ever undertaken in the steel bathyscaph trieste they set out to descend to the bottom of the mariana trench in the pacific a distance of over ten kilometres the particular spot they chose was already known to be the deepest in any ocean but nobody had ever dared to try to reach it no one had any conception of what they would find there or whether they would come back alive

in their bathyscaph in a space less than two metres high and one across the two men pitched and tossed on a stormy sea while the crews of the two us navy support vessels stood anxiously by at 8 33 a m the signal was given and the trieste began to drop in utter silence into the unknown depths after passing through a twilight zone then a darker zone the bathyscaph entered the abyssal zone a world of complete darkness where time has no relevance finally at 1 06 p m the trieste gently touched down on a level bed of yellow ooze piccard and walsh made a token claim in the name of science and humanity to the ultimate depth in all the oceans of the world though in fact their landing was nearly 400 feet short of the deepest point in the mariana trench the explorers were well content to rest on their laurels however and return safely to the surface

Judith Cooke

19   Work from your own punctuated passage to answer these
     questions.
     (a) What synonyms could be substituted for 'insatiable desire'?
     (b) Use the phrase itself in a sentence which will clearly illustrate
     its meaning.
     (c) What kind of exploration is called the last great frontier, and
     why?
     (d) What is a bathyscaph?
     (e) What can we deduce about its construction?
     (f) Why was Piccard and Walsh's journey one of the most
     perilous ever undertaken?
     (g) How big was the bathyscaph, and how long did it take to
     reach the bottom of the Mariana Trench?
     (h) Where does the writer say that time has no relevance, and
     why?
     (i) Explain what it means to rest on your laurels.
     (j) Why were the explorers content to rest on theirs?
     (k) Use these words from the passage in sentences of your own
     which will clearly show what they mean: frontier, embarked,
     descend, support vessel, abyssal zone, relevance, rest on their
     laurels.
     (l) Use the photographs on pages 151 and 152 to write an
     accurate, detailed description of the bathyscaph and of Jacques
     Piccard.
20   Write detailed criticisms of two of these poems.

TO ROOST

Past sundown, the west hung with heaven,
each suburb goes to roost,
each house like an obedient fowl
settles its hump in softening silhouette,
lets fall its blinds like a cluck's wings,
and broods . . .

Outside, the larrikin street-poles looped with lin
play leapfrog past the sleepers
and bounce in rhythm down the line of sky.   (cont.)

But the houses huddle, draw closer to themselves,
hug their hearths, frost nagging at their shoulders,
convinced that, for some diurnal reason,
come the dawn, they will hatch humanity again
for its day's season.

Colin Thiele

CHANCE MET

Swing back the gate till it stumbles over the furrows,
Where the plough swerves close to the fence and the brown earth
   crumbles
From mountains crested with tossed-up tussocks, to valleys
Runnelled with rivers of rain.
The drops hang bright on the wires, the diligent spider
Worked shifts all night to set up his house by sunrise
Between the hinge, rusted with rain, and the latch.

Who went before through the gate—this affable stranger
Who touches the topmost rail and leans to dazzle,
Spinning his hat for greeting? Morning,
Golden and rakish, who stole his shirt from the scarecrow
To shroud the fire at heart. Good Morning
Swing back the gate, good fellow.
Swing back the gate! There is nobody there. The sunlight
In golden footprints runs up the ridge of the hill.

Rosemary Dobson

AN OLD JAMAICAN WOMAN THINKS ABOUT THE HEREAFTER

What would I do forever in a big place, who
have lived all my life in a small island?
The same parish holds the cottage I was born in, all
my family, and the cool churchyard.

(cont.)

                              I have looked
up at the stars from my front verandah and have been afraid
of their pathless distances. I have never flown
in the loud aircraft nor have I seen palaces,
so I would prefer not to be taken up high nor
rewarded with a large mansion.

                              I would like
to remain half-drowsing through an evening light
watching bamboo trees sway and ruffle for a valley-wind,
to remember old times but not to live them again;
occasionally to have a good meal with no milk
nor honey for I don't like them, and now and then to walk
by the grey sea-beach with two old dogs and watch
men bring up their boats from the water.

                              For all this,
for my hope of heaven, I am willing to forgive my debtors
and to love my neighbour . . .

                              although the wretch throws stones
at my white rooster and makes too much noise in her damn
    backyard.

A. L. Hendricks

21   Write a lively description of the photograph.

22   Write:
     (a) a review of any book you have read recently;
     (b) a short story based on *either* a proverb *or* a local legend *or* on
     fantasy.

23   Write essays on any two of these.
     (a) Pollution.
     (b) My Ideal Sports Centre.
     (c) The Play I Most Enjoyed Performing In.
     (d) Advertising.
     (e) 'Why bother to read and write? All communication will be
     oral soon, and tapes and cassettes will be used instead of books
     and written records.' Discuss.

(f) Euthanasia: the Points For and Against.

(g) 'Napoleon called us a nation of shopkeepers. Now we are not even that, but only a nation of spectators.' Discuss.

(h) World Population.

(i) What, in your view, constitutes a successful career, and why?

(j) The Wedding.

Book List

Units 1 and 2
Dylan Thomas *A Prospect of the Sea* (Dent)
Charles Dickens *Hard Times* (Dent)
Spike Milligan *Puckoon* (Penguin)
Charles Dickens *Great Expectations* (Penguin)
C. Everard Palmer *My Father, Sun-Sun Johnson* (Deutsch)
K. M. Peyton *Flambards* (Puffin)
K. M. Peyton *The Edge of the Cloud* (OUP)
K. M. Peyton *Flambards in Summer* (Puffin)
Brian Glanville *Goalkeepers are Different* (Hamish Hamilton)
Rudyard Kipling *Kim* (Macmillan)
J. Meade Falkner *Moonfleet* (Arnold)
Mark Twain *The Adventures of Huckleberry Finn* (Puffin)
David Line *Mike and Me* (Puffin)

Units 3 and 4
A Small Book of Grave Humour, ed. Fritz Spiegl (Pan)
Edward Lear *The Book of Bosh* (Puffin)
Rosemary Sutcliff *The Lantern Bearers* (OUP)
Winifred Cawley *Feast of the Serpent* (OUP)
Geoffrey Trease *Horseman on the Hills* (Macmillan)
P. H. Newby *The Spirit of Jem* (Kestrel)
K. M. Peyton *Pennington's Seventeenth Summer* (OUP)
K. M. Peyton *The Beethoven Medal* (OUP)
Vivian Breck *Maggie* (Kestrel)
The Penguin Book of Japanese Verse, trans. Bownas and Thwaite (Penguin)
Chinese Poems, trans. Arthur Waley (Unicorn Books)
Li Po & Tu Fu, trans. Arthur Cooper (Penguin)
The Penguin Book of Chinese Verse, trans. Kotewall and Smith (Penguin)
Active Anthologies, Books 3−5, ed. Albert Rowe (Hart-Davis)

Units 5 and 6
Catherine Cookson *Joe and The Gladiator* (Macmillan Education)
John Steinbeck *The Red Pony* (Piccolo)

Elizabeth Sewell *Black Beauty* (Puffin)
Irene Makin *Ponies in the Attic* (Puffin)
Gerald Rafterty *Snow Cloud, Stallion* (Puffin)
The Puffin Book of Horses (Puffin)
Lucy Rees *Wild Pony* (Puffin)
Gunnel Linde *Pony in the Luggage* (Puffin)
Eilis Dillon *Island of Horses* (Puffin)
Monica Dickens *The Horses of Follyfoot* (Puffin)
Marjorie Kinnan Rawlings *The Yearling* (Piccolo)
Zane Grey *Wildfire* (Sphere)

Units 7 and 8
Robert Heinlein *Red Planet* (Gollancz)
Robert Heinlein *Citizen of the Galaxy* (Puffin)
Robert O'Brien *Z for Zachariah* (Armada Lion)
Louise Lawrence *Andra* (Macmillan Education)
Arthur C. Clarke *Islands in the Sky* (Puffin)
Arthur C. Clarke *Of Time and the Stars* (Puffin)
Arthur C. Clarke *Dolphin Island* (Piccolo)
Isaac Asimov *Heavenly Host* (Puffin)
John Christopher *In the Beginning* (Longman)
John Christopher *The Death of Grass* (Wheaton)
H. M. Hoover *Children of the Morrow* (Methuen)
Monica Hughes *Crisis on Conshelf Ten* (Hamish Hamilton)
Simon Watson *No Man's Land* (Gollancz)
Jane Yolen *Zoo 2000* (Macmillan Education)
James Blish *The Star Dwellers* (Faber)
Alan E. Nourse *Scavengers in Space* (Faber)
Andre Norton *Moon of Three Rings* (Kestrel)
From Frankenstein to Andromeda, ed. J. G. Brown (Macmillan)

Unit 9
Ted Hughes *Season Songs* (Faber)
Charles Causley *Figure of 8* (Macmillan)
Charles Causley *Figgie Hobbin* (Puffin)
Songs for All Seasons, ed. Rosemary Dobson (Angus and Robertson)
A Choice of Comic and Curious Verse, ed. J. M. Cohen (Penguin)
The Penguin Book of Australian Verse, ed. Thompson, Slessor and Howarth
   (Penguin)

Acknowledgements

The author and publishers wish to thank the following who have kindly given permission for the use of copyright material:

Angus & Robertson (UK) Ltd for the poems 'The Beach' by William Hart Smith and 'Chance Met' by Rosemary Dobson from *Songs for All Seasons* edited by Rosemary Dobson; Wanda V. Barford for a haiku poem first published in *New Poetry* (Workshop Press); Carcanet Press Ltd for the poem 'Blue Toboggans' by Edwin Morgan from *From Glasgow to Saturn*; Andre Deutsch Ltd for the poem 'An Old Jamaican Woman Thinks About the Hereafter' by A. L. Hendriks from *On This Mountain*; Faber and Faber Ltd for the poem 'The River in March' and an extract from 'Hay' from *Season Songs* by Ted Hughes; an extract from 'The Express' from *Collected Poems* by Stephen Spender; Victor Gollancz Ltd for an extract from *Citizen of the Galaxy* by Robert Heinlein; David Higham Associates Ltd on behalf of Charles Causley for the poem 'My Mother Saw a Dancing Bear' and a verse from 'Timothy Winters' from *Collected Poems 1951–1975*; David Higham Associates Ltd on behalf of The Trustees for the Copyrights of the late Dylan Thomas for an extract from *A Prospect of the Sea*; Macdonald & Jane's Publishing Group Ltd for an extract from *Joe and the Gladiator* by Catherine Cookson; Spike Milligan for an extract from *Puckoon*; Edwin Morgan for his poem 'Linoleum Chocolate' from *The Second Life* published by Edinburgh University Press; Betty Parvin for her poem first published in *New Poetry* (Workshop Press); Penguin Books Ltd for four senryū from *The Penguin Book of Japanese Verse* translated by Geoffrey Bownas and Anthony Thwaite (1964); Margaret Ramsay Ltd on behalf of Alan Plater for an extract from the play *Terry*; Rigby Ltd, Australia, for the poem *To Roost* by Colin Thwaite; John Wareham for his poem first published in *New Poetry* (Workshop Press).

The author and publishers wish to acknowledge the following photographic sources:

Associated Press Limited pp. 151, 152; Anne Bolt p. 155; BBC Copyright Photo pp. 39, 40; Granada TV p. 10; Richard and Sally Greenhill p. 33; Holte Photographics Limited p. 127; Eric Hosking p. 61; Radio Times Hulton Picture Library pp. 84, 132; Spanish National Tourist Office pp. 25, 26; Charles Stebbings p. 18; Zoological Society of London pp. 79, 106.

The publishers have made every effort to trace the copyright holders but if they have inadvertently overlooked any, they will be pleased to make the necessary arrangements at the first opportunity.